Ryan Talevi

This document provides exact and reliable information regarding the topic and issues covered.

In no way is it legal to reproduce, duplicate, or transmit any part of this document in either electronic means or in printed format. All rights reserved.

The information provided in this book is stated to be truthful and consistent. Any liability, in terms of inattention or otherwise, by any usage or abuse of any policies, processes, or directions contained within is the sole responsibility of the recipient reader. Under no circumstances will any legal responsibility or blame be held against the publisher for any reparation, damages, or monetary loss due to the information herein, either directly or indirectly.

Respective authors own all copyrights not held by the publisher.

The information in this book is solely offered for informational purposes and is universal. The presentation of the information is without a contract or any guarantee assurance.

The trademarks used are without any consent, and the trademark publication is without permission or backing by the trademark owner. All trademarks and brands within this book are for clarifying purposes only and are owned by the owners, not affiliated with this document.

The Complete Coin Collecting Bible

9 Volumes

The Complete Coin Collecting Bible: The Beginners' Guide to Identifying & Preserving your Collection. How to Buy & Sell Coins to Transform your Hobby into a Moneymaker, Even If You Are Just Starting.

BY
Ryan Talevi

Ryan Talevi

Table of Contents

4

3 VOLUMES

THE COMPLETE
COIN
COLLECTING
BIBLE

RYAN TALEVI

The Past, Present, and Future of Coin Collecting.
Discover Collectors' Ultimate Strategies for Investing Well
and Knowing When to Sell.

Introduction

The art of collecting coins, also known as numismatics, is much more than just an academic study of coins or paper money. Imagine how collecting coins was just one among the many hobbies of people and is now a profession that needs expertise and proper skills to derive the historical significance and current worth of coins or other currency units.

To give you a technical reference, numismatics is about collecting rare and priceless coins or currency units. The job of professional numismatists is to derive the production tech, physical specifications and historical connection of the currency or coins. Their research is what adds clarity to the honest value of rare collectable coins.

Depending on the research outcome, when the authorities find that the coin can be sold over its face value, its circulation becomes prohibited. Thus, it is then considered an investment instead of real money. If you believe there is just one form of studying money, then it is a wrong assumption!

Numismatics differs from the economic and historical studies conducted on coins or various currency units. The trained coin numismatists are responsible for deriving the physical attributes of specific payment media, especially coins. They do not interfere with the usability or contribution of those currencies to the economy.

Even though numismatics studies various currency units, we still emphasise coin collection. It is because numismatics is mostly termed as a coin collection, as this process implements intensive study than just collecting the coins.

To help you eliminate this confusion before we start this book, you must know that:

"All numismatists are collectors of various ancient and priceless coins. Still, not every coin collector can be called a numismatist.

It is because collecting coins is a hobby, and studying their integral value is a profession. So, with this differentiation, you are now aware of how this book will be approached further in the chapters. We will cover numismatics and keep coin collection as a prime touchpoint for our explanations.

So, is very interesting it to know that a team assesses coins, currencies, tokens, and other objects used for trading in ancient history.

There is more to this profession and what it has offered mankind for decades. And this Book will educate you all about it, including numismatics' past, present and future.

We thank you for buying this Book and giving your precious time to the topic: it is evident that you have developed an interest in collecting coins and numismatics. If you are passionate about being a numismatist or about studying numismatics, then this book can be accountable as a good start for you.

Read along till the end, and let's cover everything about numismatics and coin collection, starting from the past.

Volume 1

History and Evolution of Coin Collection and Numismatics

Money has been declared a rare commodity since ancient times. People were instructed and brought up with lessons on working hard to earn them. Moreover, money, especially coins, was made from scarce materials, such as bronze, silver and gold. Using such coins in the past facilitated trading opportunities for people from one location to another. It is because everyone recognized these precious metals and the carvings on them as an object of value.

As humans evolved, a legitimate problem was witnessed solely depending on coins as currency. As all coins were made of scarce metal, it was becoming expensive and difficult to transport those materials in bulk to long distances. Thus, there was an evolution and transition of currency from sole dependency on coins to the introduction of paper money.

The reason is evident! As paper was lighter and more convenient to carry, it became one of the most popular forms of physical money for a long time. Even today, it is a convenient currency mode, preferable by all. The coins continued to persist in near ancient times until the modern-day evolution was proposed.

Even with the gold or silver coins being ruled out of being used as money, they were & are still considered investment entities and objects with high value. And as the era of these ancient and traditional coins was banished, the quest of finding, sourcing, and collecting those rare and unique coins began.

Some did it out of passion and to fulfil their hobby of collecting things of the past. But at the same time, the world got introduced to the art of numismatics, where professionals started to collect rare coins and extend their research on them. They take up the job of predicting the date of production, the era when it was used, and the proposed value of it in the current era.

Stepping into the History of Collecting Coins or Numismatics

The initiative of collecting coins dates to ancient times when the world knew some astounding rulers such as Caesar Augustus. Augustus himself was a coin collector. He had a passion for collecting coins from different regions or kingdoms. He used those coins to hand them over as presents to rulers of other kingdoms for conducting trades or agreements.

Talking about the first Renaissance collector, Petrarch wrote letters that gave verdicts on how some vine diggers reached him to buy the coins he collected. Not just that, those diggers also identified all rulers, the impressions of whom were engraved on those coins. History credits Petrarch with this honour!

A book named *"De Asse et Partibus"* or *"De Asse"* is considered the first text or book published in the history of ancient coins. It was available to the world in the year 1514 and was written by Guillaume Bude. Some of the documents of the past have records on early coin collectors, which stated that most of those collectors were kings and emperors.

Some of the popular coin collectors in the past are King Henry IV-France, Pope Benedict VIII, and Emperor Maximilian-Roman Empire.

The 19th Century Coin Collecting Evolution

It was the 19th century when coin collectors started to work as professional societies. In the quest, they started producing journals to document their discovered coins. As per the statistics, the American Numismatic Society has more than 800,000 coins, currencies, and medals under its possession, dating back to around 650 BCE. Moreover, they also have a library that holds more than 100,000 books.

Modern numismatics took charge of researching the use and production of coins and currencies of the 17th century and onwards. Such an initiative was taken to determine the rare significance of all coins they studied. With the introduction of the internet and other such modern communication alternatives, studying coins became convenient. It is now easy for researchers to share their insights about ancient coins over an internet community and help people learn history easily.

1.1 Learn the Art of Making Coins

There are various parameters that make one discovered coin different from the other. It might be in terms of value, design, engravings, or shape. But as far as the research verdict is concerned, the process of producing or making coins has been the same since ancient times.

The metals selected for making the coins are meant to be abundant and scarce to ensure it replicates a considerable value. The selection of material has been varying from culture to culture and from age to age. For instance, China used copper as their coin material in the past, whereas India used silver. Things changed when the economies of different countries started to evolve.

As stated earlier, the process of making coins has been the same since ancient times. Over time, only the process has evolved, but the blueprint remains the same. We will learn more about the modern-age process of making coins later in this chapter.

At an early age, with the permission of the King or whoever was in charge, the materials were picked. In ancient times, gold, silver, copper, electrum, and all of their alloys are preferred for making coins.

First, a blank coin is made from these materials by melting and pouring them into the specified molds. The coins were either made in the shape of a disc or a long strip.

The long strips were cut down into small blocks before they could be engraved with the designated markings. The blank coins are then smoothened from the edges to eradicate all roughness.

Later, the coin is certified by a mark representing the rulers of that time or a marking representing the value of that coin. As the world was constantly evolving, this procedure was refined and improved with technology and material changes. In the modern era, coins are marked with recognized symbols and a designated value.

In ancient times, the material of the coin represented its worth, whereas, in the modern era, the value imprinted on the coin is what holds the weightage.

The stages involved in the making of the coins are:

1.1.1. Mining the Raw Materials

The minting of the coins began with the stage of mining the raw materials. Today, there are mines in all parts of the world that supply materials such as copper, silver, gold, and others for various usability.

The raw material that is collected directly from the mines has a lot of impurities. Therefore, they are not directly used for the coinage aspects. With modern-age technologies and ideologies, governments are recycling discontinued coins to retrieve the metal and produce new ones.

1.1.2. Refining, Melting and Casting

This stage is dedicated to refining the metals to eradicate all their impurities. Some of the specific types of coins demand the use of an alloy made up of two or more metals. Once the metal is refined, it then undergoes the melting procedure. When the destined alloy is achieved, the metal will then be cast into an ingot.

Ingots are large metal bars that consist of a specified weight of the metal that is required by the mint. The purity is of utmost concern, for which these ingots are thoroughly checked.

1.1.3. Rolling of the Ingot

The next process involves rolling the ingot, which determines the proper thickness. There are two hardened steel rollers that press the ingots between them. When the process is done, the ingots will then be in the shape of a strip, with a proper thickness that the destined governments require for their coins.

Moreover, the rolling process also works towards softening the metal and changing its molecular build. As a result, the metal will now be easy to strike, and the quality of coins will increase.

1.1.4. Blanking the Coins

The metal rolls are then processed to remove the curvature within the manufacturing process. It will be passed through the machine, which will punch out metal discs of adequate diameter and thickness. Hence, the coins are finally made.

1.1.5. Riddling

It is the process of separating the proper coin blanks from the waste metal blanks. It is a possibility that some impurities might have slipped through in the refining process, which might result in dirty metal blanks. Such coins cannot be used for circulation, for which they are filtered out.

1.1.6.   Cleaning and Annealing

The coins will then be passed through the annealing oven, which is destined to soften the metal, and prepare it for striking. The coin blanks will then undergo a chemical bath to remove dirt or oil that might be stuck on the surface of the coin blanks.

1.1.7.   Upsetting

Once the cleaning is done, then the blanks enter the upsetting stage. Here, the blanks are again passed through a small roller setup, which is used for imparting a metal rim on the coins for either side. Hence, this will perfect the diameter and make the coin ready for a stamp strike. Once the upsetting is done, the coin blanks are then termed as planchet.

1.1.8.   Stamping

As the planchets have undergone preparation, cleaning and softening, they are ready to be stamped or struck. In the modern world, there are coin-pressing machines that take in these planchets and give out perfectly stamped coins. With such a machine, more than a hundred coins can be pressed in just a minute.

The proof coins that are made for collectors undergo the hand stamping process. The dedicated person in charge will feed the planchets to the press and give at least two strikes for each coin, to get the stamp right.

1.1.9. Distribution

Once the inspection of coins is done, they are all set to be distributed for circulation. The coins are filled in bulk bags and then shipped to the Reserve Banks of designated countries. The coins are then further distributed to banks.

On the other hand, the collector coins are kept in special boxes and are sent to various coin collectors across the globe.

1.2 Coin Collectors

1.2.1. Who Takes the Mantle of Collecting Coins

The numismatists are the professionals who take up the mantle of collecting coins. Numismatics is the study of coins that you all already know. There is no specific name for coin collectors apart from this professional designation. Coin collection is also described as the hobby of kings and emperors, which indicates that this has been a pastime for a long.

Among all coin collectors of the past, one of the early names is Augustus, the Roman Emperor. Later, an Italian antiquarian, namely Bartolomeo Borghesi, established scholarly science to introduce numismatics. He also catalogued several coins in his collection, including the Vatican coins made for Pope Pius VII.

Some famous names who collect coins are Paul McCartney, jack Blac, President Donald Trump and Nicole Kidman. They are not numismatists but have the passion and urge to collect unique and rare coins by considering them art or investment.

1.2.2. Reasons Why Coin Collection Satisfied both Professions as well as Passion

Collecting the coins is a kind of artwork. Numismatists do it to respond to their profession calls, but they have a deep interest in this hobby, which leads them to dig deeper into the rarity of those coins. As stated earlier, collecting coins satisfies both passions as well as profession. Not everyone can be a numismatist, but everyone who has the urge to collect coins doesn't have to.

Your reason might be different from Ig started with collecting rare coins. Whether you want to study more on the rarity of those coins, buy it as an investment or just seek personal enjoyment, it is your call.

Coin collection is fun! They are little treasures that have a lot of stories hidden within. People treat them as art that feels good to look at or set up on display. You will find a lot about them written in history books. The ancient coins were once used for trading goods, running politics, and managing kingdoms. There is nothing that isn't fascinating about these collector coins.

Some people take this hobby up for investment or enjoyment, while others go deeper than that to research its existence and production and become numismatists. Irrespective of whether passion or profession interests you in coin collection, let's talk about all possible reasons for it to be something worth collecting.

- **Coin Collection for Education and History**

The first and most important reason for collecting coins is the rich education about the history that it unveils. Historians, numismatists, and passionate collectors learn about the dates it belonged from, the culture it showcases, events when it was used, rulers who distributed them and the significance of the symbols.

Today, almost every archaeology excavation site reports the discovery of ancient coins from across the world. The introduction to the coinage system commenced in the 8th century BC, for which the extreme ancient sites did not have such signs of ancient coins. Now, you get to know this only when you dive deep into the hobby or profession of collecting coins.

Don't you have a question in mind, like, what did people use for trading before the introduction of coinage? Probably you do! Hence, this is the terms of education that you will receive in the long way of acquiring coin collection as a hobby or profession.

The answer to the question is that, before the introduction of coins, the barter system was used for trading. In this system, goods or services were exchanged as money or payment for trading with one another. It is a very old method, which continued until the coins were introduced.

Like this instance, there are many more lessons and educating historical evidence, which makes coin collecting even more fascinating. Many coins from the medieval period have the date engraved on them, along with the name of the rulers under which the coins were distributed or used.

People with a fascination for learning the history of coins will find it intriguing to learn how things are executed. A chronology of all historical events is linked directly or indirectly with the coins being used in that era. Hence, studying the coins will emphasize your knowledge of how various things were executed in the past.

The metal composition used in making the ancient coins gives a verdict on the empire's economic condition in that era. For instance, Muhammad Ghori, in his time, stamped the impression of the goddess Lakshmi on the gold coins of his era. Alongside that, he also got his name engraved on those coins. Hence, upon discovery and research on these coins, it was evident that Ghori was religious and worshipped the Hindu goddess.

Just like that, the coins don't just reflect the value it holds, but it is a projection of the achievements, dynasties, events, places, and logos. All of it and more were meaningfully expressed through the coins that were used in the past. Thus, coins are considered a crucial inscription in world history.

Coins are considered the sole evidence of how trading functioned under the rule of various kings. The purer the material, the better the financial condition of that time. Some of the inscriptions on coins even reflect the territories that the kings have conquered. As the history books were written with factual and documented evidence, these coins are the proof for all information that has ever been derived from literature.

It has been more than 3000 years since humans started using coins for selling, purchasing, and trading services and goods. The coins are also stated as an early mode of communication by rulers of respective states. The inscriptions or engravings on the coins were meant to send out a message to the masses.

There is more to the history of coins that you should learn and cherish. And people with a passion towards deriving this knowledge either become numismatists or collect coins to dig up their theories. They have the liberty to explore the rarity of these ancient coins that have been part of the human trading culture for thousands of years.

- **Coin Collection as Hobby and for Relaxation**

The second most thought about reason for collecting coins is when you have a hobby for it. For some people who are fascinated about historical evidence, would love to collect coins and cherish its ancient uniqueness forever. People with the hobby of collecting coins, do not prefer to use or trade it for investment or money. Instead, they write books, theories, and blogs on how unique the coins in their collection are.

Whether you have a hobby of collecting art pieces of the past, or to understand the trading system of rulers, the coins are what would be a perfect fit for your exploration journey. Even the kings of the past considered it a hobby to collect coins. It is a hobby that can last for a lifetime, as there will always be new coins for you to collect. There are several ways for you to be a coin collector, with endless possibilities.

The hobby reached the United States in the era of 19950s or 1960s. People could find coin shops in around every corner of the country. The coin collectors were welcomed to trade their rare pieces for a befitting amount in return. Some of the coin shops were owned by collectors. But as there was a massive economic downturn, the American coin collecting markets experienced a halt in 1980s and 1990s.

The hobby started to fade for quite a time, due to the introduction of video games and high-tech gadgets that kept people busy. There were only few among the many who held onto their passion of collecting coins and continued their quest to find the rarest coins available across the world.

Apart from making it a hobby, people are also intrigued to collect coins to relax themselves and free their minds from stress. It is proven that assembling and studying the coins and their origins can potentially relieve you from pressures and stress for the day. If you find any coin store nearby, you can buy the unique coins to add onto your collection and study them to fulfil your quest of attaining relaxation.

Today, internet is full of stores that are selling legitimate coins of the ancient times. Thus, if you have the urge and money to spare for increasing your coin collection, then internet can be best used for the purpose. Beyond that, you can also attend the coin shows, and go for the ones that are on sale. But remember, coin collecting is an expensive hobby, and you might have to pay a value that corresponds to the uniqueness and time stamp of the piece you intend to buy.

So, if you want to do it for fun, then keep your budgets in consideration while you collect coins.

- **Coin Collection for Earning Money**

Coins also function as a mode of investment in today's world. Coin collectors who are specific towards earning a fortune out of their unique collections know this. Ancient coins made of gold or silver, with historical evidence will add immense value to your investment portfolio. You need to have the skills of assessing the genuineness of the coin before you can buy and use it as an investment.

There are many experts that will give you a verdict on how precious bullion metal coins are. You need to get coins, the value of which you know will increase with passing time. You don't want to risk the investment strategy you have built out of coins. Moreover, the best thing about treating coin collection as an investment is that you can liquidate them at any point of time. If you are in need for cash, you can put up the coin collection online, or head out to a coin shop.

There are hundreds and thousands of passionate coin collectors out there, who would give you your asking amount in exchange for the coin. But remember, if you are strict in this pursuit, you must understand the rare coin market in depth. Be familiar with the coins being discovered, put up for sale and other such factors. Just like any investment asset, the rare coins also have demand fluctuations. Apart from that, the coins that are available for sale can trigger positive or negative effect on the prices.

So, you must be educated enough about the coin collecting quest and be aware of how its market functions, if you want to use it as an investment asset. It has been a significant consideration for quite a while now. Even though most of the coin collectors enter this arena for the historic, artistic and cultural significance, but some consider it a way to earn financial freedom and acquire money.

You need to be extremely smart to invest on particular coins that you believe will return you the profit in the long run. It is a dream for almost all coin collectors or investors to come across one such rare coin in the market, that can lead them to make millions. There are some rarest coins in the entire world, owned by some of the reputed coin collectors. And it is next to impossible to convince someone to let go of the priceless possession.

So, getting a rare coin to trade as an investment is a pipedream. Therefore, you can start by owning the demanding coins, and get good scope of monetary returns out of it. Patience, smartness and awareness is all you need to make efficient sales and purchases. Take note of the legal guidelines as per your country or state on buying or selling the rare coins.

There are two ways of making money out of the coins you have collected so far. Either you sell one coin that has a rare value in the market or sell off your entire collection to a coin shop for liquidating them into cash.

The rare coins are considered investment because they have less or no risks. Unlike stocks, you won't find the price fluctuations varying from a peak to crash, when dealing with the coins. They are tangible assets, and you can earn a great lot of money, as the value of coins appreciates over time.

So, this is one of the evident reasons why you should collect coins. If you want some tips to get started on this journey, then here they are:

1. Take your time to learn the rare coin market and become a student for any series of coins.
2. Get your insight into some of the best coins to collect.
3. Get your coin collecting supplies such as coin scales, tongs, microscopes, coin magnifiers, etc.
4. Build a good relationship with coin dealers.
5. Always remember to buy at a low price and sell at a higher valuation.

- **Coin Collection as a Goal Accomplishing Challenge**

One more reason why people are keen on collecting coins is the fascination to accomplish the desperate goals. Finding, sourcing, and collecting the rare coins is a challenge for everyone. And when you have taken up coin collection as a designated and serious hobby, you tend to have a goal in mind to fill up your collection with specific coin series.

It has been a thing with many coin collectors who are in this field. Even the professional numismatists also express their views on how they were keen on collecting rarest coins in their times when they were just collectors.

All the successful coin collectors establish a goal in mind of what coins or series they need to collect for themselves.

Keeping that in mind, they decide on different sourcing methods to find and locate the coins. It might be in the coin shop next door, or across international borders. And this is the challenge they are ready to take up, for fulfilling their quest of collecting desirable coins.

When finally, the coin you are searching for is sourced and collected, you will feel the satisfaction from within. The thrill you cherished for hunting down the coin and fulfilling the established goal will all be justified when you complete the challenge of collecting important coins.

- **Coin Collection to Cherish the Art and Beauty**

You got to agree on the fact that every ancient or rare coin has artistic impressions, which is a skill that is not so common across the world. The astonishing fact is that people in the ancient times were capable of making molds with such top-notch designs. Today, there is technology to speed up things, and artists to design curated coins, based on government's and Reserve Bank's guidelines.

In the past, the artists with a brief knowledge on bas-relief sculptures. Artists work towards making bas-relief by sculpting a specified figure on a 2D plane. The output gives a

3D appeal which is skillful enough to be visible from all sides with just little or no distortion.

The profession numismatists have given their statements that the most beautiful of all coins that they have seen are the double eagle coin of the sculptor Saint-Gaudens in the US, which was made in between the years 1907 and 1933.

A true coin collector who has experience in studying the history of rare coins will be able to see and cherish the artistic beauty of these coins. Even in the coins that dates back to thousands of years, you will see fine artistry in terms of inscriptions. You can see every minute detail with fine edges, which explains the importance people gave to their jobs in the ancient times. The skills they possessed has been passed on and taken over by the technologies of today.

People collect coins to present its beauty to the world by showcasing them in their collection racks. You will find any coin collectors who have dedicated rooms in their houses to create a museum-style display of these coins. They be the guide for people to decode the artistic impressions on each of the coins. For a true admirer of antique coins, the art and beauty are the sole reason to get along with the hobby of collecting coins.

- **Collecting Coins for Making a Long-Lasting Impression**

With a strategic investment of time, efforts, and money on collecting valuable and rare coins, you can make a long-lasting impression among your colleagues, friends and family members. In today's era people flaunt their financial achievements, which are commonly available for every rich family to avail. But this cannot be the thing with antique, ancient, and rare coins.

There is a high chance that the coin you own in your collection, is the last of all that was minted back in its time. Even with all the money people have, they cannot buy a second piece of the coin that you own. And this is when the coin you collected becomes priceless. When you meet your work colleagues or fellow coin collectors, you feel pride in telling and showing them your rarest collections.

In this competitive world, fame and recognition comes to you when you do or show something that can leave a long-lasting impression in the minds of people. And obtaining that rare coin that almost all coin collectors were rushing to buy is something that will set you up on a limelight. Whether you use the coin as an investment asset or a collectible trophy, it is up to you. But your people will remember you for leading the quest of coin collection and bringing in the rarest of coins within their network.

- **Collecting Coins to Pass it Onto the Future Generations**

What's better than leaving your priceless possessions for the future generations as a valuable inheritance property? As the value of rare coins appreciate over time, imagine how valuable they would be for your future generations. You need a very strategic planning on what coins to buy, what to hold and what to liquidate, to have a good collection to pass onto your next generations.

Remember, it is not like a lottery that you can collect coins overnight and become rich. It takes time, patience and sheer dedication to plan out investment strategies on valuable, rare and antique coins, to ensure it would appreciate over time. When you do this, you will have a vast collection of priceless coins to pass onto the future generations as a worthy property.

Apart from that, you should also take your time to help your kids learn the importance of these ancient coins and how valuable they are. It is to ensure that they take care of the collection and keep adding up to the collection in the future. Share the same wit and passion you have for collecting coins, with your children and tell them to pass it onto their offspring.

It is your legacy that you will be leaving behind in the form of coin collection. And people will remember you for it!

1.3 Coin Collection Methods and Approaches

After the introduction of coins in the 8th century BC, the coin collecting hobby came to existence in the 12th century. And since that day, it is a very popular hobby for people from across the world. As professional numismatists collect coins to study on their antique and unique appeal, the passionate collectors do it to satisfy their challenge, admire the beauty, leave a legacy, make an investment or just to attain a satisfaction.

It is said that one of the best ways of collecting coins is to save and preserve them. For instance, try and source some coins that you saw as a kid being used by your parents, but are now valueless in terms of Reserve Bank, but are demanding in the coin collection market. The lower value coins of the past can be a demanding and collectible coin in the future. So, if your old storeroom or a wardrobe drawer has some valueless coins, pick it up and store it somewhere safe. You don't want to regret losing them when you realize the value of it in the long run.

Holding onto all varieties of coins that exist today will also become rare in the coming times. If you can add few of them to your collection, there will be a time when the value might escalate. And if you get bored of waiting, you can always spend them for the value they have in the open market. But holding onto the coin is an art! As stated earlier you need sheer dedication in terms of reaping the true value of a coin.

For some people, collecting coins is not just a hobby but is a passion of collecting rare artifacts. So, the method that we discussed above can't be applicable for such rare coin collecting fanatics. Therefore, to ensure you know the right approach on collecting, preserving, and cherishing the coins, this section will elaborate on various methods, ways and approaches you can adapt to satisfy your quest of collecting the rare artefacts.

To help you get started with your coin collecting quest, here are few of the practically tested approaches, that even the numismatic experts suggest. Coin collection is an art, and you need to take adequate steps to make it reap benefits for you in the long term.

Let's get along with the methods:

1.3.1. Start with a Simple and Small Approach

If you are not a rich lad, you don't want to make mistakes in buying the wrong coins, or investing in the artefacts that won't give you the returns as you expected. Even though you are not collecting coins as the purpose of investment, you still need to pay an amount to get most of the coins from stores, internet, or coin shows.

Unless someone gifts you a rare collectible coin, you will be always buying them. So, the best approach for the start is to buy small and pick simple coins. Go with the smaller coin sets that are available in the shops and make small purchases. Don't buy all the coins in a series just because you are a fanatic of coin collection.

If you want your collection to mark an impression for you, then you just need the rare ones and not the entire lot. Don't buy something that you can't sell off in the future when you realize it was just a hasty purchase.

Visit the coin shows that are mostly held across various countries and states. Pre-define your budget and stick to it while you are going from store to store to buy your set of coins. If you have a good budget in hand, you can start off with type sets of coins with some research on what's valuable and demanding in the collection or numismatics market.

1.3.2. Collect the Coins You Like

One among the many methods for you to collect coins in your life is to just go with what you feel like collecting. There are many types of coins out there that are rare and unique in their own ways. Not every coin might hold a special value in the market, but the rarity can't be turned down for those coins. Do your bit of research and find some coins or series of coins that you feel like collecting.

Do you already have one coin from a popular series with you? If yes, then why not make up your mind to collect the rest of the coins and complete the series? You need to first determine what interests you about a coin! There is a total of more than thousands styles, patterns and designs of coins, which varies in terms of size, date, origin, age, uniqueness, ancient connection and other such parameters.

Well, while this task might seem daunting at first, but will eventually help you get clarity on how you would approach your passion of collecting coins. Remember, there is no mandate on always collecting coins from the past.

If you are not passionate about the antique coins, you can just decide on collecting coins from each year, since your birth year till the year you will die. If not that, you can plan on collecting the lowest or highest value coins of all countries you could explore in your lifetime. It is upon you to pick the style, series, and pattern of collecting coins to help make it easy for yourself to get started with your coin hunt.

The above examples of coin collecting ideas are easy to hunt. If you feel like such ideas won't challenge you from within, and won't be satisfying your passion, then dig deeper to find the favorable series of coins from the past. If you have an age or date in mind, then use it and search the internet for all possible coins that have unique value and rare significance of that time.

As a coin collector, you need to have the right tools to verify genuineness of the coins yourself. It is because, there are many counterfeit coins available in the market that are masked and being sold as original. Try never to buy the rare coins from online markets, as determining the originality becomes difficult in such cases.

When you have finally made up your mind on the coin that you want to collect, why wait further? Learn a bit more about it from the educational resources, to ensure you don't make expensive mistakes in buying or recognizing them. In your quest of collecting and buying coins, you might come across many vendors who will try to sell you off high-significance coins at bargained rates.

There is a high chance all those coins are fake, because a genuine dealer never has to approach the customers for buying their coins, as the passionate collectors come to them anyway. You should stick to the choice you made and collect just those coins about which you have studied enough to make no mistakes. The last thing you should know while collecting coins out of your own wish is that you should always buy from trusted dealers with reputation in the market.

1.3.3. Set Your Coin Collection Goals and Execute Your Plan

Not everyone would like to go blind on collecting coins, based on their likings. Some do have the intention to collect valuable coins, for sake of being rare or for being rich in the long run. If you are one among them, then it is advised you should prepare some goals for yourself and then work on creating a roadmap or plan to achieve them, with respect to collecting coins.

While you are making plans, there are certain things that you should keep in mind. The things that are discussed below are advice to ensure that you are walking down the right path and are adapting the right method to acquire the desirable coins.

So, the things you should keep in mind are:

- **Don't Count on Coin Collection Journey as a Race**

It is understandable that you want to add more worth to your personality and be the owner of rare and antique coins. You need to be patient enough to source all those rare coins and work hard to collect them for yourself. You cannot rush to get things done, as you won't be able to source all the necessary coins from one vendor, or from a single coin show. When you hurry in your path of collecting coins, you will tend to get frustrated soon, and will possibly give up on the passion of collecting coins.

Moreover, when frustrated you will start to lose money, either while buying the coins or while selling off the coins. So, make sure you are studying well about the coins you have made up your mind to purchase, by considering their value and rarity. Take your time and determine how to distinguish between the original and fake coins of that type, study about the history & availability of it and try to source it for a purchase.

It might either be with the coin vendors or Individual collectors. When a collector like you owns a rare coin that you need, there is a very less chance you could convince him/her to sell it to you at a good price. Hence, this is why you shouldn't race your way in coin collection journey. You don't have to be frustrated if the rarest of all coins is not available for sale. You can always try various other sources to look out for more of those coins. You just need to have knowledge on where to look for your required coins.

Just the opposite consideration of this fact, imagine you are getting a rare coin very easily at the first coin store you landed in. But there are scratches and dents all over it, which is degrading its value. So, will you just take the coin because it is rare and is available in the first attempt representing your luck?

You shouldn't just fall for the first coin that comes your way. There will be more, and you need to wait for the quality that you seek as well. When the quality and pricing requirements are met, only then can you consider buying the coin and add it to your priceless collection.

- **Join Some Coin Club**

While you are on your quest of planning to collect coins because you are passionate about it, you can prefer joining a coin club for the same. One among the many ways to learn about coins is by being around the people of same kind. If you need a proper plan to start with, spend some time with like-minded people and you will start thinking like them, to attain success in sourcing the best coins. There are many clubs across the world, both physical and virtual, where people share their coin collecting stories, talk about availability of rare coins, trade the coins and much more.

Among the members of these clubs, there are many numismatists as well. They share their brief studies on specific coins, share ideologies on how to collect several coins and explains the rarity of them as well. There are coin clubs that are divided in terms of categories as well. It means that if you are fond of a specific series of coins, there might be a coin club with members that shares the same interest. Joining such groups will help you stay updated with all latest coin show events, newly sourced rare coins of the series and much more.

It doesn't matter If you are a beg"nner'or an expert, the clubs are open for all to explore the beauty of history in the face of coins.

• Have a Budget in Mind

Preparing a plan and chasing coin collection goals without a budget is a very dull approach. So, make sure you do some research and determine the base amount of money you will need to collect the coins you are looking for. There might be some showstopper coins which fascinates you but are at a higher cost. You don't have to stick to them right from the start, as there are many rare coins out there that are affordable for you to buy and will still give you a long-lasting impression.

You should set a budget and direct your research of coins according to that. Prepare a spreadsheet and specify your budget on the top. Now, if you have read books on most valuable and unique coins, then you can refer to them and check the price range of coins within each series. List them down in an ascending order to determine how many coins you can target on purchasing within the budget that you have specified. Eventually, you will either include or exclude some of the coins that you prefer to have in your collection.

Now you must decide whether to go for an increase in budget to get just one coin that went off charts while preparing the spreadsheet or buy multiple other rare coins for now. The one that couldn't be bought can be obtained sometimes later, but forcing yourself to increase the budget right from the start is something that will set you up on a wrong practice.

Mark the coins that you couldn't buy due to short of budget. It is just a matter of patience and good times. When you can spare enough money to buy the coins you couldn't the first time, you can go for it. Keep the sheet tabs checked for the coins that you have bought already. It is to ensure that you don't buy duplicate coins in the future.

1.3.4. Follow the Pre-Specified and Effortless Techniques of Collecting Coins

It is true that there are endless possibilities on how you head out to choose and collect the coins you like. There is no way that all those possibilities can be framed under one book. Therefore, the officials and professional numismatic experts have set up some pre-defined rules on how you can collect the coins at ease, without wandering around the bush, or paying too much money unnecessarily.

The ways are as follows:

- **Buy the Slabbed Coins**

Some of the professional numismatic experts have already obtained certification and grading for specific coins. They are called slabbed coins and are made available from the third-party grading firms. These coins are then housed in an air-tight container for preserving the rarity and uniqueness of it.

As a coin collector, you can buy such slabbed coins at pre-defined rates, without the need for auctioning or bidding for anything. The numismatists have done the major job for you, and a lot of rare, valued coins are available for you to buy.

- **Collect Coins Based on the Mint and Date Mark**

The mint and date marks on collectible coins indicate the mint facility where the coin was stamped, and year when it was ready for distribution. It is again an easy way of finding and collecting the coins. There are any mints that produce certain coins at a low amount, to see how they circulate among the people. Later, when the production is shut down for such coins, they automatically become rare.

So, a little bit of research on such coins will help you identify the easily available coins, that most of the vendors will possible be having with them. As per the US and other country governments some of their respective coins with specific mint and date marks are considered rare and has high value. So, you just must do your research and identify them all.

- **Collect Coins Specific to Region**

One of the most favorite means of collecting the coins in all numismatic community is by narrowing down your preferences based on the regions. When you look out for specific coins as per your preference, it is better to narrow them down as per the region. Determine the region, such as if the coin is from US, Asia, Canada, Australia, China, or other parts of the world.

Specifying the region will help you as collectors to pick your specific niche and direct your research efforts towards it. In this way, it will become easier for you to collect the specific coins.

With all these methods, you are evidently aware of how to start with your coin collecting quest. But, if you want to take this hobby as a profession, then you must count on studying numismatics through online or offline courses.

If you want to pursue the profession, then you must earn a diploma or M.A. degree in numismatics and archaeology. There will be several courses within the curriculum of your degree that will include subjects to teach you the fundamentals of detecting the coins, grading them, altering them and modern-day minting procedures. There is a vast scope of earning fortune out of this profession, as modern-day archaeologists and numismatists are working together to discover the hidden secrets of human civilization relentlessly.

It is very common for the archaeologists to discover ancient coins time over time, which is then sent to numismatists for further analysis. When working the archaeological departments, you will get to fulfill your passion of assessing the antique coins and earn for your contribution towards the service. Your job will mostly be to determine the date, their production period, and the usage in terms of historical context.

Coin collecting as a hobby or as a profession is quite interesting!

This section was all about giving you a glimpse at the history of numismatics and coin collection. When you aren't aware of what triggered this hobby to be such a big market in the modern days, you won't be able to direct yourself in the right path to be part of this journey. It is an interesting and challenging hobby or career that allows you to look at the past and know about how the evolution happened over time.

Whether you are fascinated about the coins that you used while you were child, or the ones that your ancestors did in their time, collecting all of them would give you the satisfaction from within. As we get to know about our past heritage due to the popularity of this hobby, people aren't going to stop exploring their ways of getting hands on some of the rarest coins.

You must know that the rarest of all coins that have a high significance is mostly examined by numismatists and stored in the museums across the world. They are not for sale or private collections as it is considered as the property of country's government. There is a very rare chance that governments would ever auction their priceless possessions which represents the history of mankind and country.

So, when you are researching for the coins that you want to collect, filter out the options that are beyond your reach. And remember not to fall for the trap set by fake vendors who care to sell you counterfeit coins of those rare museum pieces. You might have to limit your passion of collecting coins to the ones that are available for sale across the countries. Coin shows, auctions and stores will help you with book of rarest coins that are available for sale, and the ones that you can get from them.

When you have good relations with reputed coin vendors, they can help you source a lot of your favorable coins without charging you a fortune.

<u>Volume 2</u>
How to Make Money through Coin Collection

Coin collection is not just a hobby or passion for someone but is also a means of income for some. People tend to collect the rarest of coins and wait for its value to hike over time. When the price is finally risen to their satisfaction quotient, they tend to sell it to the potential buyers.

The sellers of coins were at time the buyer of the same collectible item. It means that the rarity of coins won't fade away if the value has increased for it over time. Therefore, you will always have a list of potential buyers to get that coin from you, but you need to hold onto it until the price satisfies your inner conscience of profitability.

You just must look for the buyers at right platforms, and you won't have to spend much time finding the sellers. But all of it is a strategic process of execution, without which you might end up buying the wrong coins, selling to the wrong buyers or end up losing on the market value.

So, in this chapter, you will know how to make money deeper through your coin collection approach. Take a note of each step, and make sure you master them all in order to acquire the best possible value.

How to Make Money through Coin Collection

Before you take an insight into what coins are worth collection, you should understand what makes them valuable. There is no such necessity for a coin to be valuable just because of its age. For an instance, you can own some Roman coins that are more than 1500 years old, but the value of such coins is less than $20 in the coin market.

Age might be one of the many factors of determining the value of a coin, but the major consideration is always given to the demand and supply. When demand is high and supply is low, the value will hike for the coins, and the value will drop if the situation is vice versa.

Some specific coins, such as Mercury dimes or Buffalo nickels, are much more popular than others with the same denomination. As a result, more and more coin collectors are looking for those popular coins, which ends up increasing their market value. Apart from scarcity and demand of the coin, the condition also holds utmost importance in specifying the value.

There is a possibility that the coins from the earlier era might have been produced in high volume in comparison to the same coins in later date. Therefore, the older coins might still be available in the market for buyers to attain. Hence, this is how supply factor is measured! But it isn't expected for all those rare or high demand coins to share the same value, because the condition is yet to be assessed.

It depends on how many of each of the coins of that age has been saved, and in what condition. If the state in which the coin was under preservation hasn't been effective in preserving the textures and denominations over it, then the value will be deteriorated.

Following that, one more factor that determines the value of coins of the same date is whether they are circulated or uncirculated. Uncirculated coins tend to have ten times more value than that of the circulated coins. It is because, you can be sure of a flawless condition for an uncirculated coin.

2.1 Coin Grading System

2.1.1. Understand the Grading System for Determining the Worth of Coins

Grading is the measurement process for determining the state of coin's preservation. In most of the cases, you can conclude that, higher the grading metrics of a coin, the rarer it is, or vice versa. And rarity means increased value of the coin. Higher grading is mostly allotted to the coins that have their original appearance and design intact, just like uncirculated coins.

But, as most of the series of coins have undergone extensive circulation, the grading is allotted accordingly, based on the quality parameters set by professional numismatists. It is difficult to source uncirculated coins, which would be possibly in best quality, and would easily get high grading status on them. The buying value for such coins is often higher, but so does the selling cost in the long run, making it ideal for you to make ample money out of it.

People who are collecting coins as hobby often bypass the grading consideration at most instances. They stick to their budget and preference for collecting coins. Not everyone has a lot of money to spare on buying collectible coins! But, to ensure that you get a good value for a purchase you make today, grading is one of the prime considerations that shouldn't be neglected.

Therefore, to educate you on descriptions on all circulated grades and detailed aspects of proof and uncirculated coins, let's dig deeper into the grading assessment.

1. Circulated Coin Grading

Circulated coins are ones that have been used to some extent throughout the daily commerce of the specified time. Due to this factor, there is a possibility of some wear, as many people must have handled it differently.

As scarcer and older coins are quite rare to be found in an uncirculated condition at the mints, these circulated options are considered better to meet your needs. But, even when buying the circulated coins, you should take note of the grading scale.

Under circulated grading, the categories under which the coins are marked for their qualities.

- **Good:** Coins that have a readable date with full rims are considered 'good'. For a circulated coin to be graded as 'good', it should have a completely retained design outline.
- **Very Good:** Coins that have a complete rim with retained definitions, and clearly visible numerals and letterings, are graded as 'very good'.
- **Fine:** A coin with moderate wear is acceptable under this grading. The date should be bold, and all legends & letters should be clear. The major elements of the design might showcase some separation, and such quality obtains a 'fine' status.

- **Very Fine:** If only two-thirds of the overall coin's design is clearly visible with letters and date having sharp definitions, then the coin can be termed as 'Very Fine'.
- **Extra Fine:** When all the design elements are clearly visible in a coin, with just the high points of a design being worn out, then the coin can be graded as 'extra fine'.

2. Uncirculated Coin Grading

Uncirculated coins are specified for the specific series of minted coins that never went into circulation. Such coins are often stored for several years within the mint-sealed bags or are carefully and sincerely preserved by well-known coin collectors. As a result, there is no chance of any wear, caused to those coins due to the general circulation of usual coins.

As a lot of coins are kept together in a single bag, the only possible signs you will see will be of the bag, atmospheric aging, physical contact with other coins, staining or blemishes. But even with the signs that cannot be reversed, these mint-stored coins will remain uncirculated, as they are of the best possible quality, and poses scarcity.

Most of the uncirculated coins are graded with parameters ranging between MS-60 to MS-63. There are very few uncirculated coins that matches the technical standards, specified for MS-65 or higher than that.

3. Proof Coins

Proof Coins aren't graded, as they are specifically made for collectors to preserve. It is more like a method of manufacturing special coins, made from special process over chosen coin dies and blanks. They undergo rigorous burnishing and polishing process to eradicate all forms of imperfections.

Once finished, the proof coins again undergo critical inspections to meet the specific standards. They are to be handled only with gloves and are packaged properly for being delivered to the collectors.

2.1.2. The Metal in the Coins

Talking about assessing what makes a coin valuable, there has been a common belief among coin collectors that the metal is responsible for increasing or decreasing the coin's value. For instance, silver and gold coins represent value in two different ways. They have their collector or numismatic value and precious or intrinsic metal value.

Coins that are of high grades will have a valuation assessment with respect to higher premium than that of their metal value. But at the same time, the coins that are of lesser grades won't be getting that privilege in their value assessment.

2.1.3. How to Pick a Coin Series that is Worth Collecting for You

Now that you know what makes a coin valuable, it's time you take a closer look at how you can pick a specific series that seems worth collecting for your passion. Over several years, mints from across the world have produced various coins that were circulated for quite a long time. You might have a book of coin series listed in brief for fueling your passion on what to collect and what to omit.

Open the book or any informative resource you own, and pick the options of coin series, the design of which you admire and the composition of which interests you. Once you are done with thigs part of shortlisting the series of coins you might want to collect, move onto the next step of narrowing down the list further. Now, research upon the popularity of each of the shortlisted coin series.

Soon, you will have a couple of series that you have prioritized among the rest for your coin collecting passion. As you now know their popularity and market value, buying it will be worth your time, as making money out of them in the long run might be a profitable play.

It is up to you to either choose one coinage series, complete it and then move onto the next, or work on multiple coinage series simultaneously. When you finally end up buying or collecting coins that are worth it, you can just treasure them as your priceless property for generations to come. If not, then wait till the value peaks and sell them off at a whopping price.

2.1.4. Find a Professional who Could Help You Determine a Coin's Worth

You can connect with any professional numismatist or a coin company for assessing the rarity of a specific coin that you own. If you just want the information on specific coins, you can still ask about the value of a coinage series or a particular coin, which will help you decide if it's worth it to start your hunt for collecting it.

Apart from that, you must also try and learn from the professionals on how you can properly handle or store the coins to maintain their natural condition. Appropriate care is also one of the key necessities for you to ensure you get an optimal value over time when you sell it. Some of such valuable handling tips for collectible coins include:

- Always hold the coins by edges, to protect the front & back sides of it from natural oils in your fingers and fingerprints. Fingerprints or the natural oils can be corrosive for the coin over time.

- As a passionate coin collector, you should make it a habit to use cotton gloves while handling the uncirculated, circulated or proof coins.

- Improper cleaning has always led the uncirculated or circulated coins to experience avoidable damages. Inappropriate cleaning methods can deteriorate the original mint-style color and finish of the coins. As a result, the value of your collected coin will be lost forever.

- Even if you intend to get the coin cleaned to determine its actual condition, then get it done by professionals.

- When you store the coins, make sure the space is free from high humidity, salt air, extreme temperature, or air pollution. Prefer to store them in areas where the temperature is uniform.

2.1.5. How to Sell Your Coin Collection

There is an art of selling almost everything, and your collectible coins are no different. You must have clear idea on what you could expect on selling your coins. Whether you want to sell your coins yourself, or prepare them for a widescale sale, you need proper understanding on various parameters.

First, you need to get all your coins grades and get them priced fairly. Following that, you need to find all the potential coin dealers who might be interested in a specific coinage series or coin. Once you sell the coins, keep a record of it. You can also choose to hire a professional for selling all your coins, but you will have to pay a commission for it.

By handing over the job to professionals, you needn't to bear the hassle of finding dealers, auctioning the coins, grading them or other such aspects. The experts will do the needful. The only thing you need to make sure is that the professional coin selling company is charging you a fair commission. If you are paying too much as commission, then you will be losing a great margin on the profit earned.

In addition to that, some countries have taxation rules on everything that you sell for earning profit, and coins are no exception in this case. Therefore, validate the taxation laws with any official, to have a general idea in mind on how much would be your net profit after selling the coins.

The steps might seem very direct and easy for selling your coin collection. But it is equally complex to ensure that you are getting an optimal value for the coins you sell. It is a natural instinct that you would like to keep all of the profits to yourself, except the mandatory tax that you have to pay. You can save the cost of hiring professionals, if you are aware of all the practical considerations you should make before selling the coins. So, this step is all about educating you with those measures you should take in between owning and selling your coin collection.

Considering that you have decided and bought the coins that are worth the value as graded and assessed, how to finally make money by selling your collection. Here are few of the crucial things that meant for you to implement in order to get the maximum value out of your collection and make your investment profitable.

2.2 Collectors' Strategies for Making Money

One of the most prominent strategies for collecting coins is to pick the rarest coins of high quality and grading. You must get your coins graded by numismatists or other licensed professionals, to have an idea on how much price you should sell it for.

But even before that, you need to study about the coinage series that fascinates you the most. Even though you have collected them all, based on their value and popularity as referred across the online resources, you still need to learn a lot about those coins, to determine how rare, they can be in the coming times, and what will be the expected value.

Studying on a specific coinage series will help you know if all the coins within the series are rare and valuable, or only a part of it is worth collecting. Hence, you can either get rid of the coins that don't add value to your collection or hold onto them for selling them as a whole series in the long run.

Apart from these assessment strategies, expert coin collectors have also requested all of coin fanatics to buy necessary supplies to check the quality themselves. Although your grading won't be considered legal for pricing the coin's value, but a general assessment would help you prioritize which coin you can sell for an optimal value at what time.

Therefore, make sure you have coin magnifiers, loupes, coin tongs, coin scales, coin calipers, microscopes, handling kit, preservation chemicals, and much more. Now, take a special course on how to use these supplies for assessing your collected coins.

These were few of the strategies that expert coin collectors suggest for you to ensure you make a lot of money out of selling your coin collection. A rightful assessment is all you need, both before and after you buy the coins.

2.2.1. Best Time or Finest Moment for Selling off Your Coin Collection

Selling your entire coin collection to make money is not an easy job to do, as it takes years to collect all of those priceless coins that have futuristic value. But what's difficult is not impossible! To ensure you get the maximum value of your entire collection, you need to be patient enough with your eager to get liquid money in account.

You have spent quite a long time in building this collection, which demanded you time, money and effort. And, selling it all out for pennies will not be a good motivation for you. So, make sure you have the knowledge to sell your coins at the right time only. It is just like stock trading, as you get great opportunities for profiting out of buying and selling the assets. But you need to determine the proper time to acquire that benefit.

Similarly, the best time to sell your coin collection depends on various factors. One of which is when the metal prices seem to be high. This is applicable only if you own silver or gold coins in your collection. For other minted coins, you should look out for the steep rise of market value for a particular series or coin. It will be an indication that the supply has fallen while the demand has risen. Thus, it might be the right time for you to sell off the coins.

Unless you don't have any financial emergency, it is better to give it time, knowledge, and research before selling your entire coin collection.

Country officials often organize some numismatic gatherings to discuss everything related to the coins. These gatherings also host several events such as auctions, classes, and other such special sessions. It is considered an optimal time for people to sell off their coin collections. It is because, these gatherings are held in pre-summer and post-holiday months. Currently, people seem to be more relaxed and in better mood to invest in rare and high valued coins.

Apart from that, there are five questions you should ask yourself, to decide if it is the right time to sell of your coin collection.

The questions include:
    a) Is there any financial challenge?

If you are in some kind of financial challenge such as debt consolidation, urgent unavoidable rent dues, or any health emergency, then it's better not to wait for the right time and sell out the coins for liquid funds. It makes no sense to hold onto the coins, while your life becomes miserable without liquid money.
    b) Does it feel right to let go off all the coins?

Most of the coin collectors decide on selling off their existing collections to buy more coins. They sell off the coinage series or specific coins that they no longer need, or are of less value than the others they own. But what if a valuable coin is in stock with the nearest dealer, and you suddenly must sell off a large chunk of your collection to get it.

In that case, will you find yourself to be ready to let the coins go off, while you welcome the new ones. It takes time to assess your collection for filtering out the coins that hold importance and the ones that doesn't. In all of a sudden situation where you have to buy the one coin that you have been waiting to acquire for so long, you might have to take a decision on selling off random coins that you think aren't of great value.

Moreover, if you are just selling the coins to earn a good lot of money, even then you have to bid farewell to your entire sets that you collected with ample time, effort and money. The years of hard work will be gone! So, even if you are selling the coins for money, you still need to be mentally ready for emptying your collection.

c) Is it right to wait too much for selling off the coins?

Is everyone around your network with similar coinage series are selling off their coins? Are you afraid that too much supply being created in the coin market, will eventually drop the value of this coin in the long run? Should you still hold onto it or sell it right away?

You need to find answers for all of these questions. Do detailed research on whether a dealership is buying the maximum coin of similar set, or are the trades being done between two collectors. It will help you understand whether the supply is being increased in the market, or the coins are just being transferred from one collector to another.

It is because, if the supply increases in the market, the demand will be met, and the prices will fall for the specific coins. And, as coin selling is also a volatile market just like stocks, you never know when will the price return to the position where it was the last time. So, if you feel like the prices are going to drop for a particular series of coin drastically, due to its minimal scarcity and sudden increase of supply, then it's better to sell it off with the mass.

2.2.2. Deciding what's the Best Price for your Coin

The next in the line of what things you should keep in mind before selling off the coins is what would be the best price for your coin. The best price of your coin is to be decided by what you believe is a satisfactory profit count against the price you paid while buying it.

Depending on the rarity and supply aspects of a coin, you will be charged a price higher or lower than what the market is dealing in. Suppose a particular Roman coin is high in demand, but the supply is very minimal. In that case, the coin dealer or the owner will be asking a hefty price for selling it to you. In contrast to that situation, if the supply is very high, and the demand is moderate, then the buyer will have ample options to look for the same coin at cheaper price.

In such a situation, the seller will be at loss, if a genuine buyer doesn't take on his/her deal. Therefore, they reduce the price in comparison to the market, to ensure that the sale is done.

You got to understand how you decide on what would be the best price for a single piece, a set or your whole collection. We believe you have taken a record of every penny you have spent over collecting coins.

If you are just a beginner or rookie coin collector, then you might not be feeling the necessity of keeping track of your expenses in terms of coin collection, but over time you will regret this decision.

It is because, if you come across some emergency or just want to refresh your collection, you need to know at what total amount you spent for buying the entire sets of coins. Following which, you can set up your selling bid by deciding on your profit percentage. You cannot expect the buyers of your collection to consider that. It is your collection, and you have to add your profit cut to it.

Therefore, even if you are a beginner in coin collection, make it a habit to take note of all expenses you make. In this digital era, preparing an online spreadsheet won't cost you a penny! Keep making copies of it or keep a physical record of the printouts of your older collections, to ensure it will be accessible anytime you want it.

Coming back to the report, pull it out at the time you want to sell off a single coin or your entire collection. If you are selling a single coin, then find the recorded amount you paid for buying it. Once you do, quote the selling price accordingly with a room for negotiation, without affecting your profit cut.

If you are selling online, then quote your price accordingly, or if a buyer has walked up to you buy it physically, keep your room for negotiation short, as you don't want to sell it off in loss. But, at the same time you must also consider what's the current market value of the coin. If the supply is high, and the demand is degrading over time, you might have to cut down on your wider profit window and shorten it to just complete sales. In contrast to that, raise your prices high, if there are only a few coins of type available in the market, and you own one of them.

In this way, you can determine what's the best price for your coin, and how you should put it up for sale, without compromising your profit window.

2.3 Ways of Selling Your Coin Collection

Before selling off your coin collection, one of the most important things you must evaluate and consider is the varying ways of how you could sell them off. Well, as of today the technology and use of digital platforms have been beyond excellence. But coin collection has been a trend since long back, when there was no form of actual trading that we know today. So, as we intend to sell off the coin collection for making a great lot of money, it's important to be able to determine all possible ways of selling them off.

Here are some of the most convenient and highly preferred ways collectors use for selling their coins:

a) Selling to a Coin Dealer

The first thing that would come to your mind when you think of selling your coin collection is to reach out to the dealer who has helped you attain most of the collections. They have a detailed knowledge on how demanding a particular coin is at a present moment. And if you have good relations with the dealer, then you ought to get a good price out of it. But, if you are approaching a completely new coin dealer for selling off your coins, it is advised you take quotations from a few of other dealers too.

Get an insight into what different coin dealers are ready to offer you for the same coins. When you find the deal with maximum price being offered, you can finally sell off your set of coins. But one problem with the dealers is that you can expect them to buy only a single set or a couple of coins from you. But if you intend to sell your entire collection which has over hundreds and thousands of coins, then a dealer might not be able to afford your deal or buy it all.

You might have to look for dealers who are extremely rich in their profession and have turned around the coin collecting business into a million-dollar sector. But even then, you cannot be assured of the fact that they would show interest in buying your entire collection. If you have such fascinating options in your collection, then some dealers might give you an offer. But do remember that assessment of your profitability is important when you are selling the coins in bulk. So, this is one evident way of selling off your coin collection.

b) Selling it to a Legacy Coin Collector

Coin collection is not just a hobby, but it has been a legacy for many families. Some of the families have been collecting coins for several generations. Such people are born rich and want to dedicate their passion towards investing in collectible coins. It adds pride and reputation to their names. People of such class don't buy coins to sell it off at the time of emergency or to cash them for financial expenses.

As you are willing to sell your set of coins, you are not among such group of coin collectors. But you can definitely pitch your offer to them for buying your set of collections. Take an appointment with them and settle down to discuss on what coins you own, and where you got them. It is better if you have a picture file of all the coins that you own, with the necessary description underneath them. It will help you put up a strong pitch and convince the buyer to take all of your collection.

Even if they don't agree for buying all, if your specific coins have historical and priceless significance, they will still be buying most of them. The price percentage is merely a concern for such legacy coin collectors. What they need is the priceless value of a coin, and they would agree to the price you quote them. Remember to be reasonable on your price quote, as the person you are pitching is also a collector. So, you want to build a good rapport with someone of that reputation, to be able to sell off your coins in the future, if you continue with your coin collecting passion after selling off the existing batch.

c) Sell it Online

Today, there are various online platforms that are allowing you to be a prime seller of collectible coins on their platform. A lot of buyers are exploring these sites to buy specific set of coins at best rates. If you own quite a lot of them, then you can run ads over the website, at a nominal cost. In this way, your coins will get a wide global exposure, and you will be able to bid your preferred rate for a good profit count.

There are various platforms online that offers the same kind of a service, but you need to pick the best of options where most of the reputed and high-society buyers look for coins. Check out the ratings and reviews to understand how genuine and feasible the platform is. Pick a few of the options that are better than others and start listing your coin collection over the platform.

Now, if you have hundreds and thousands of coins, as you have been collecting for a long time now, it will be difficult for you to list all the products, one-by-one over the platforms. What you can do is hand over the job to professionals. Hire a couple of freelancers and pay them to list all of your coins within the collection over the dedicated websites. In this way, you will be having no commitments with those freelancers, and you can pay them to end the service once the job is done.

You can put up one ad to sell off your entire collection for sure. But in that way, you will be abided with only option over the platform for buyers to consider. You will be closing the window for people who want to buy only a couple of coin sets from you. Not all buyers would feel convinced of the fact to buy the entire collection to get only a few of the sets that they want. Therefore, individual ads are quite important over such platforms, to have more options on earning money out of selling coins.

Now, all you have to do is wait for the offers over these platforms and see if someone is initiating any negotiation. If you have room for negotiation, be open for it or set off the conversation with your final offering. If the buyer places an order, you will get a notification for shipping out the same, after you get the money credited in your account.

As simple as it sounds, the more complex it can be, if you don't price the coins as per market value. If the buyers find your coin expensive, they will report your pricing, and all your other coins might not be noticed due to the same impression. And, if you are pricing it too low, people will buy it from you and sell it over the same platform at a higher rate to dump your profit percentage.

So, make sure you study on the market demands of each coin at present, and update the same in your report. Make sure you enter the right amount as the coin market suggests now. You will eventually be getting a good flow of sales, and the profitability won't stop either.

d) Online Auction

It is more like the previous way of selling your coins, but there are dedicated platforms designed for online auction. You will be uploading the ads of your coin collection, and people will start bidding on it. You will set the base price, and people will try to win it over by a higher bid.

You will be setting a bidding window, within which all the interested buyers will have to place their bids for a particular coin, a set, or your whole collection. Once the window is closed, you will be assessing all the offers, and find the one with highest bid. Sell off the advertised coin collection and get the amount. It is that simple when you are using online features.

But the catch is, you must have valuable coins to put up for auction. The ones that are easily available with dealers or at online coin stores, won't get high bids. Apart from that, you should also keep a reasonable base price, after studying the market value of all the coins you are displaying for an auction online.

If you want to draw attention of more and more buyers to your coin, make sure your collection is worth the hype. The online auction house also charges a percentage for every ad that gets sold over the website. Suppose you have three ads for your three different coin collection sets. In that case, you will have to pay the decided percentage of the selling price three times, to the auction house.

It is considerably fair as the online auction house will give a wide network exposure to your coin collection. So, if you sell through their network, paying a small price out of the profit won't trouble you much. But, if you sell it outside of the auction house, and are de-listing the coin from the online hub, then you might not have to pay any charges.

e) Combine all the Above Ways

These were the three of the most practical ways of selling your coin collection and earn money out of it. But the best way of speeding up the process of selling your entire collection is to combine all of the three ways mentioned above. You should go to a coin dealer first, then connect with a legacy coin collector and list the collection online.

Firstly, get all of the coins that you want to sell, listed on the dedicated platforms. What would happen is your coins will start getting the exposure it needs. And there is a possibility that you will get some good offers to compare your profitability with other selling options.

Suppose you have listed the coins and are now heading to a coin dealer. The coin dealer offers you a specific price for a particular set of coins, but at the same time you already have a higher offer from the online platform for the same set. Now, you can use the offer to convince the coin dealer for matching the price or go beyond it to ensure your profitability.

Similarly, approach the legacy collector too, and don't talk price with them! Instead, show them the popularity of your collection that the coin dealers and people online are highly demanding it. Show them the demand of your collection, and they will be convinced to buy it at a greater price than what both coin dealers and the online buyers are about to offer.

You can then de-list the ad for a particular coin or set, from the platforms, and then repeat the process for other sets in your collection, whenever you plan on selling them.

2.3.1. Display Your Coin Collection

Among all of the things in this section of what you should know before selling off the coins, this stands the last yet the most important point. You must know how to display your coin collection. Suppose you are inviting a few of the collectors or dealers to your home to show them your coin collection and pitch them to buy it, then you should at least be presentable to showcase how valuable the coins are.

The best way to display your coin collection is by using a shadow box. Now, you can set it up in a way that the light's focus prioritizes your favorite and the most expensive coins. Apart from that, you can also consider buying a display box that has a velvet base across all racks. Get some coin holders from online or offline markets, that has a soft material. Now, treat the storage surface of the display box with any available solution that would not affect the texture, imprint, or the design of your coin over prolonged storage. Install small lights on the outside and place some on the inside, to make sure they add more elegance to your presentable display.

When you are able to display your collection well, people will have the urge to check the condition of coins more closely and will eventually be convinced to buy them. If you believe, you have the best of coin collections that are highly demanding across the world, then you can also host an auction, by taking help of a professional firm that is an expert in hosting such bidding events. Call in the famous and popular coin collectors or coin fanatics, to bid for your majestically displayed coins.

So, make sure you work on the displaying aspect of your collection, as it holds utmost importance in showing your passion towards coin collecting. When your fellow coin collectors whom you pitched about selling off your collection know that you have maintained the quality of those coins over time with good care, they might be ready to pay the amount you have asked with respect to its value.

Volume 3

Collect as Investment

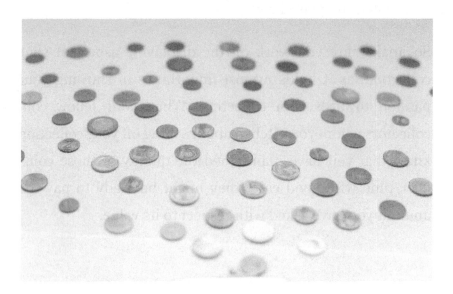

The best approach for earning money out of your coin collection is by considering the purchases as an investment. We have been discussing this throughout the book several times now, but with this section of the book, you will get a clear understanding of how coin collection turns out to be profitable as an investment.

As per the research and data insights, it is proven that a typical investor or coin collector holds onto his/her collection for at least five years before selling it off for a profitable amount. In an assessment report from 1979 to 2016, the average annual returns for coins of all types under the MS65 category was 11.0%, whereas for coins of all types under MS63 to MS65 was 9.3%.

In this comparative assessment of returns on coins against stocks, gold bullion and treasury bonds, only stocks had a higher annual return percentage over the coins, with 12.6%, whereas all of the other investment assets had a lower percentage.

The rare coins are breaking the market, as the index shows an average increase of their value by 248% within the past ten years. Auctions around the world are contributing to the increased investment capabilities of rare coins. Rare coins, being part of the Rare Tangible Asset strategy, are considered the best options for achieving privacy, market performance, currency protection, portability, and other such perks, just like investing in any precious metals.

To help you understand this, you must know that rare coins lie under the category of asset class and are not co-relation to any other traditional assets within the mainstream. Therefore, this coin market also remains unaffected due to the downturn movements or volatility that persists in all the other markets.

The records state that in the past, only rich collectors or speculators showed interest in this market and made their investments. But today, with coin collection becoming a hobby, passion and popular mode of investment, the rare coin market is much more accessible than it ever was. Today, it can be part of anyone's investment portfolio without much hassle.

Collecting coins as an investment is more like a combination of profit potential, non-correlation, and stability. With such characteristics, rare coins come together to become one of the most important assets for people to invest in. If you are looking for something to back up your other investments while you gear up your performance by investing in other viable assets, then a rare coin collection is something that stands perfect for you.

When you are buying a coin as an investment, you need to look after various assessing parameters, which include:

- Outlook of the coin
- Number of similar coins that exist in the market
- Number of similar coins with similar/better condition that are available in the market
- Price or auction history of the coin
- Places to sell off your coin at the best possible rates.

Do you have an insight into all of it? If you are just starting off with your coin collection habit as an investment, you have probably missed out on assessing one or two of these factors stated above. But, as this chapter focuses on helping you make money out of your coin collection, this step or section of this chapter shall help you get answers to all the processes involved in collecting coins as an investment.

Each of the sub-sections below will educate you on detailed parameters of what you should know to make maximum money out of your quest for coin collection as an investment. So, let's get along with it.

- **Understanding Coin Market Trends and Values**

The investment portfolio for coins varies depending on the client's individual needs. The coins that are truly rare with a high potential for growth in the forthcoming years can be acquired at a value ranging between $5000 and $10,000 per coin. But with detailed research on how the coin investors are approaching their investment strategies, most of them aim for an average investment on collectable coins of $50,000 to over $100,000. Thus, it is a great number for people who are strategically sound and are way proficient in terms of assessing which rare coin would go upward and which is not worth investing in at all.

But, for a start, you should stick with the minimum-valued rare coins at best. It will help you understand how the market functions. The profit cycle should continue to grow, which will further help you increase your investment amount or buy more coins over time. All the rare coins are determined over the open collectables market, which has no controlling bodies. The coins being bought or sold across the world will affect their prices of them in the free market.

The value will rise for your collection, as the collectors and investors will be paying more amount for acquiring the rarest of coins. The rare coins have been collected in the past and used as a wealth backup for centuries. The condition of rare coins that have survived so long to this exact point cannot be restored back to their original form. Hence, this aspect of rare coins makes them even more desirable. Thus, if there are specific coins that are found in mint condition, people will pay for them crazily over time.

Collecting coins as an investment is more like a commodity, just like a few others. You won't find an abundance of them available in the market, and the supply of those mint condition or rare uncirculated coins is also being suppressed day by day. But, seasoned investors are more engrossed in learning, assessing, and validating the worth of coins to determine the ones that are way better investments in comparison to the traditional methods.

Alongside the popular perception of coin collection as an investment, people still believe that one needs to be wealthy enough to get started with this investment journey. But this is not at all a reality. Yes, there are coins that have a high asking price at marketplaces or auctions, but the returns they give are way beyond your expectations. But you don't have to break your bank to get started with such coins right away. As suggested earlier, go slow on your investment practices!

Look out for the coins that might have a good supply but are rare in terms of quality. Get hold of them! They will be available at a very fair price and will give you good and considerable returns in the long run. Collecting coins as an investment demands you to hold onto them for a long term, ranging between 5 and 10 years. During this period of time, all you have to do is sit back and watch your rare coins grow in terms of value.

3.1 Where and How to Sell Your Coin

In the world of RTA (Rare Tangible Assets), where people mostly count on assets such as classic wine, jewellery or cars, rare stamps and coins are also an integral part of the category. The same is recognized across the world. Unlike luxury assets, rare coins are easier to buy, own and sell. RTAs are considered the best asset class for you to invest in, as it performs well, as tested over time.

Some of the benefits that you get from investing in RTAs, especially rare coins, are:

- Leading edge over inflation, as you will have bought power protection

- A combination of stability and profitability is something unique and impression with rare coins
- Coin collection as an investment is a growing market
- Rare coins are open-ended products that don't intend to fix or cap your returns to any extent.
- The cost structure is quite competitive, which ensures optimal returns.

Now that you own a set of rare coins, your next motive would be to sell them off for profit after five to ten years of holding onto them. When it's time to leave the coin investment market, the rare coins have the potential to offer you complete liquidity if your timing is right. The first thing you should consider is to look out for the right pricing. Unless there's an emergency, you shouldn't decide for yourself to get out of the market. Instead, wait for the time when it's right to head out.

You are now well-versed in the benefits of acquiring coins as an investment and have finally bought and owned them easily. Consider the right time is here when you should look out for your options to sell them out. As stated above, selling your rare coins is much easier than any other RTAs. So, here is one of the best ways using which you can sell your coin and the right procedure on how to do it.

3.1.1. Selling Coins through the Coin Dealer

One of the best ways to sell out a rare coin collection that you bought as an investment is to find the right dealer. There are steps you should follow in order to sell off your coin collection and get the worth of your investment. The steps are as follows:

- You need to first compile the entire investment inventory you own with your rare coins. You can take the help of professionals in terms of guiding you in the process. Thus, this will help you determine what pricing seems right for selling off your entire rare coin inventory.

- Following that, you should continue with professional help or take the quest into your hands to find the right coin dealer. You should look for one that has good recognition in the coin-buying or selling market. Expertise and honesty should be traits for you to consider while looking for a reputable coin dealer.

- Get in touch with at least two dealers to determine the varying values of your collection. Tally it with the market price and your determined inventory price. There is a possibility that you might not get the value as per the exact estimation you made, but it might be close.

- If you have a coin investor, mate, take a referral for connecting with the third dealer for any high price expectation. You can take a closer look at American Numismatic Association (ANA) for finding a list of all reputable coin dealers.
- Once you have your preferable coin dealer, you then have to decide your approach towards selling the coins. You can either put up a cash offer or consignment deal or ask them to organize a public auction.

Taking a Cash Offer from the Dealer

Putting up a cash offer is the fastest method, where the dealer will make an offer for your rare coin collection. The deal they offer will often be lower than what your investment should be worthy of. Even though this is the fastest approach for selling off all the coins, it is not a substantial way of getting true monetary returns. Even if you want to use this approach, make sure you have two to three offers that compete with one another and help you decide the best among all.

Setting up a Consignment Sale with the Dealer

The consignment approach will demand a month or more to sell off all your rare coins. You need to trust your coin dealer enough to hand them over all your rare coins that they will be putting up for sale. It is upon the coin dealer to set the structure of selling the coins, whereas the pricing decision will be mutual. The dealer will charge a fee from you for conducting the consignment sale.

Ask the Dealer to host a Public Auction

If you have an extremely rare or high-valued coin collection, you can ask your dealer to host a public auction. This approach will take the longest time, right from start to finish. It might even take around six months to finally sell off all your rare coin collections at the best possible bids. Both sellers as well as buyers will be paying a commission to the coin dealer in the public auction approach. The only drawback to this approach is that some of your coins might get sold at a lower value than their intrinsic value.

3.1.2. Selling Coins through eBay or other eCommerce Marketplaces

Apart from selling your coins through a dealer, you can list them yourselves over various marketplaces such as eBay,

Amazon, etc. Everyone who has engaged with these eCommerce marketplaces is aware of how to list the products and make them available for sale. There are millions of customers actively shopping for various items through these marketplaces. Listing your rare coin collection over it will be an add-on consideration for coin collectors who are always searching for options under that category.

It might be an easy process, but there are certain things you should keep in mind while listing your rare coin investment collections online, which include:

Quality Photography

Once you have created your account over the dedicated eCommerce marketplace where you want to sell your coin, you need to get photos of your coin collection that you want to list for sale. There's nothing that matters to you the most than getting the highest possible dollars for your precious investment coins. And to ensure that you are sending out the right pitch, let your quality photos of the coins do most of the talking.

The quality of the coin is what would help you acquire the highest value. So, make sure you are using good cameras for clicking photographs for your entire collection. The precise definition of textures and texts over all the coins should be clearly visible. If you own a professional camera, use it, else, call in a professional for a day's photography session. Let the professionals do the needful and give you elegant pictures of your coin collection.

Even if you own a professional camera, make sure you spend enough time learning how to use it. In this way, you won't have to spend money on hiring a professional.

Title and Product Description

Be sure of the fact to add a correct title to the coin that you are listing on the eCommerce sites. The name of the coin, its type, its category and the set it belongs to, will add a great emphasis on drawing the attention of buyers. So, make sure your title is correct, following which you can head out to write the product description.

Be honest with the product description. Take a closer look at your coins and describe the condition in brief. The areas where the imprints are fading away, or the corners that are somehow chipped, everything should be mentioned in the description. All the distracting or attractive characteristics of coins should be mentioned in brief.

When you are being accurate with your information, it will help your buyers know you are a genuine coin investor or collector. Thus, they will be helping you in the long run! The buyers will know what to expect from the coins they buy from you, and they will give good ratings and feedback, which will help increase the buyers' exposure to your collections over time.

Pricing

Identify the coin you are about to sell and derive its wholesale price in the market. Use respective books to see what price it's worth in the current market scenario. The wholesale prices are often around 50% to 70% of the retail prices. You need to give average pricing to your coin, which most of the other coin dealers are using to list their collections.

Moreover, the best way to determine the pricing for your coin collection is to grade it accurately. There are online grading tools available for you to use. If not, you can use a grading guidebook for an accurate grading journey. If you are a beginner in collectable coin investments, then make sure you take the help of a mentor or professional in this industry for it.

Remember not to over-grade the coin collection, as experienced buyers might just recognize it. If they find that the coin you have listed is over-graded, then they will mostly shy away from it. Eventually, you will have to price the coin lower than its actual value, which will put you at a loss. For worse, it might not even sell. You need to make the buyers trust you. If they don't, then they will reject your coins, even in the future.

Adding Multiple Coins for Sale

Instead of adding single coins for sale over the marketplaces, you can try adding multiple coins in a single listing to sell out your collection faster. Suppose you have a specific set of collectable coins that holds utmost significance in the coin market. In that case, why not list them all together in one sales ad?

If you have the intention to make faster money out of your coin investments, then this is an ideal approach to follow. There are many potential coin collectors who are ready to invest big bucks in acquiring a complete set or series of coins. It might take a little more time to be sold than an individual coin. But eventually, if you have given the right description and the rare coin series or set does have a significant value, it will be sold at good pricing.

So far in the book, you are already aware of the fact that if you have invested in old and rare collectable coins, you can get hundreds and thousands of dollars when you finally liquidate them. If you are a newcomer to this numismatic world, it will be a challenge for you to sell them all off. Using the above methods will help you, but everything takes time. So, try and be patient in completely liquidating your collection.

3.1.3. How to Minimize the Coin Collection Taxes?

Coin collection is a very rewarding investment idea that is gaining rapid popularity across the world. Some passionate coin collectors have generated great wealth by collecting rare and old coins that are worth the value. Even though this is a profitable investment scheme, the taxation rules are still imposed upon them. One cannot overlook the tax consequences on the profits you earn upon selling off your coin collection.

Irrespective of whether someone is collecting coins as a hobby, passion or investment, the collection will be considered a capital asset, which will be abided under the respective income tax rules. As per the laws, the gains that an individual makes out of selling a capital asset are often categorized either as short-term or long-term.

Long-term capital gains have a lowered tax rate in comparison to those short-term gains. Long-term gain is specified when the rare coins you own are sold at higher pricing than what it was a year back. In accordance with that, the long-term capital gain tax rate for the collectable coins or any other assets is termed as 28%. Being an investor, if you are selling off your coins at some loss, then you can consider offsetting the losses against your capital gains, which includes your stock gains throughout the year. Thus, you will be saving taxes.

As per professional accounting policies are concerned, you need to follow certain rules and regulations to comply with the taxation laws while trading your coin collection as an investment. The consideration policies include:

- You need to decide whether you are a hobbyist or a coin investor. Following that, you must properly and accurately report the sale of your coins while filing income tax returns.
- You need to maintain the records of purchases and sales of all collectable coins you own. You can consider maintaining them digitally or keeping a manual record of them all. The record should specify details on what coin you purchased, from whom, and at what price. While you are maintaining the records, make sure to staple the purchase invoices along with them.
- While maintaining the accounting records, you should also include a detailed list of all the coin holdings.

- Considering the value of the coins, you should get insurance for all of them, which is not a tax recommendation but a general investor's practice.

For calculating the capital gains tax that you must pay for your coin investment returns, you will have to first determine the adjusted basis. Adjusted basis is the price that you paid for purchasing the coin, which will be inclusive of the transaction fees or restoration expenditure. But, if the coin is some kind of gift or you own it by inheritance, then the basis of it will be determined based on the fair market value.

All type of collectable assets is listed under Sec.409(m) and other such regulations. Special kinds of netting rules are imposed onto the collectable's gain for determining the tax amount in a year. The tax rate often ends up being higher on the gains that you acquire by selling your collectable coins. Therefore, all the coin investors, practitioners or taxpayers often implement various strategies to reduce the overall tax paid on their collectables gains.

Some of the strategies that you can use to minimize the capital gain taxes on selling off your coins are:

- Consider selling off the coin within a year. In this way, the sale will be considered a short-term gain. Hence, all the short-term gains are taxed with respect to the usual income. So, if you have a standard tax rate of lower than 28% on your income, then you will eventually be paying less tax on your gains made by selling the coin collection.

- Donate the coin to charity rather than selling it. It is true you won't be getting any money in return, but you will be receiving a tax deduction made valid for charitable donations. The coin you passed on will not be a capital gain but a charity. The exact deduction amount will differ with respect to what the charitable trust does with the coin you passed onto them. If the charitable trust uses the coin in its work, then the deduction amount will be very high, which will match the market value of the specific coin.

If you are holding some rare collectable coins with you that are worth a lot of money if you are holding them for quite a long time, then you should consider paying the taxes and keeping the rest of the gains with you. Shortcuts on saving tax might be legitimate, but you will eventually lose out on the overall profits that you could have made. Therefore, make sure that's not the case for you.

3.2 Steps to Maximize Returns and Minimize the Risk from Coin Investment

At the end of the chapter, here is a brief insight into what you should do in terms of maximizing the returns of your investment in collectable coins and how to minimize the risks associated with it. These two factors are important considerations to help you be ready on earning the maximum possible money out of your coin investments. Without proper risk assessment and filtering out the techniques to earn maximum returns, you will eventually be missing out on realizing the true worth of your collection.

So, here is the list of steps you should follow or keep in mind while expecting returns from your coin collection. Take a closer look at all these steps to maximize investment returns from your coin collection:

3.2.1. Assemble a Balanced Investment Portfolio

Irrespective of the investment approach, diversification is of utmost importance, which will reduce the overall risk of losing out money. With your investment portfolio of rare collectable coins, you should also add up a variety of standard demanding coins. In this way, the market fluctuation will be suppressed, and the returns will be maximized.

Some of the standard coins that you can add to your rare coin investment portfolio include large cents, early quarters, early domes, silver dollars, early nickels, and half cents. To ensure more balance to your coin investment portfolio, you can also invest in gold bullion coins. These coins range from $1 gold coins to the $20 double eagles, adding more diversification to your investment portfolio of rare coins.

3.2.2. Get Knowledge on Coin Collection before Investing in Them

The best advice one can give you for maximizing your returns out of coin collection is to acquire sufficient knowledge about the approach before stepping into this investment line. You need to fully understand the investment aspects of your coin collection, which will ensure that you don't make mistakes in choosing or buying the right set of coins for making money.

This entire book is about educating you on coin collection and how you can approach it to attain profitability. Apart from going through this book, you can also talk to a mentor who has been into coin investment for a long time. Talk to them about any queries or questions to ensure you don't make expensive mistakes in the long run. In the end, stay updated with numismatic trends over the internet, and keep yourself updated with taxation, pricing and other such fluctuations for specific series of coins.

3.2.3. Avoid all the Price Bubbles

The rare coin market might be less volatile in comparison to other asset markets, but it still has certain market fluctuations that you shouldn't neglect. The prices of your coin are purely determined based on the demand and supply. Suppose there is a sudden discovery of a horde of coins that were considered rare a few years back then suddenly, the price of it will drop as the supply has increased to meet the demand.

At the same time, if there is a scarce supply, but the demand for a coin suddenly increases due to any possible news, trend or historical evidence, the price of it will increase stupendously. Thus, it means that the price of a coin can be higher one day and go down the other day, depending on various factors. You need to do your bit of research to ensure you don't get trapped in the price bubble and end up making your losses.

3.2.4. Buy Only the Quality-Certified Coins

All the rare coins that you purchase as an investment should get a certification by PCGS (Professional Coin Grading Service) or NGC (Numismatic Guarantee Corporation). Apart from these two widely known certification authorities, ICG (Independent Coin Grading) and ANACS can also certify the quality of rare coins. The latter options are not that big market players in the rare coin market but are genuine in terms of their works.

There might be two identical rare coins that might have similar grades but look different from one another. Hence, the coin that has a higher visual appeal gets a higher price than the one with the same grade but a lower appeal quotient. Even though the dealer has put up the same price for both identical and similar-graded coins, then you will eventually be going with the one that looks shinier and fresher than the other. These coins get the certification, and you will have a better chance of earning big when you sell them off.

Certification also ensures that you don't end up buying counterfeit coins that might lead you to bear immeasurable losses. Therefore, make sure this consideration is of utmost priority for you.

3.2.5. Acquire Rare Coins Privately or from Coin Shows

Collectable coins are not like any bonds or stocks, where every share you invest in is the same as that of the other. Two identical rare coins might have the same grading, but they still might be different in terms of appeal, imprints, texture, date, etc. Most of the rare coins are traded privately and not in public auctions. So, it's better to have a professional numismatist in your team who will do the work in sourcing the rare coins for you to add to your collection.

Some of the big, reputed coin shows, such as the FUN (Florida United Numismatists) or ANA (American Numismatic Association) World's Fair of Coins, are some of the known places for you to find some exceptionally rare coins. If you have knowledge of which coin sets or series hold an added market value and have the potential to grow, you can obtain them easily to use them for your monetary advantage.

3.2.6. Long-Term Growth of Portfolio

Collectible coins have the characteristics of consistency and stability in their price appreciation over a long time now. There is a long track record of performance which dates back several decades. Therefore, it is advised that people should hold onto the extremely rare coins for the long term. Do not break your investment portfolio for fear of the slightest market fluctuations. Consider the statistic, study the coin's history, and check out other considering factors before deciding on if it's the right time to liquidate the coin.

If not, then it's better to carry forward your coin collection investment for the long-term. If it is rare, then there will be a steady appreciation in the price over the forthcoming years. You can be sure that the coin is rare only by determining when it was first used, minted, or discovered. If it seems confirmed by the research authorities of the numismatists that there is no uncirculated horde of that coin found, or it is declared rare, then you can acquire it and hold onto it for a long term.

But, at the same time, keep a tab on the trends related to that coin or series of coins. In case there is any sudden fluctuation that drops the rarity of the coin beyond the bars, then it's better to sell it off or replace it with something rarer. Long-term investment will never go in vain, especially with collecting coins as an investment. If you have diversified your portfolio as suggested in the early steps, then a loss borne by one coin will be recovered by the others.

So, this is all that you need to know to help yourself earn money by investing in the rare coin market. Investment has always been beneficial for investors only when you are strategic with your moves. You might be a great stock trader, but that won't help you with the coin market. The coin market might be steadier than the stock market, but sourcing, buying, owning, and liquidating the coins at the best price is something that needs just more than skills.

The amount you earn depends on how wider risk you are willing to take. You can either take low risks by investing in safe collectable coins for a longer period to get substantially increasing value, or you can take high risks for highly rewarding investments for short-term holding durations. It totally depends on your call of what you expect to earn out of your investment and how much risk you want to take for it.

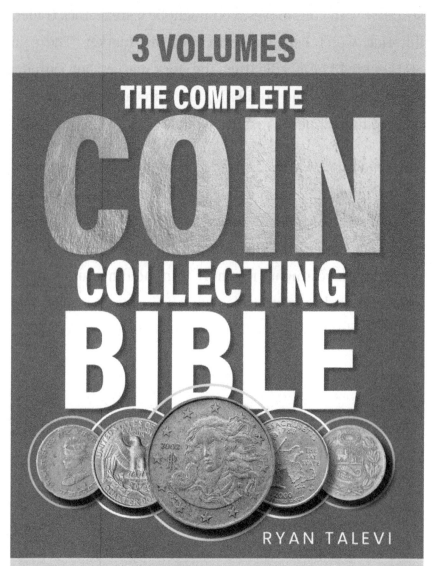

Volume 4
Where to Locate the Coins and How to Buy Them

Collecting coins is no more just a hobby for people. It's much more than that! It is a scope of investment, a legacy that people want for their future generations, and a curiosity towards learning about ancient and historical coins. With the chapters before this, you are aware of the coin collection history and how you can use them for your investment ideologies. But we wanted to dedicate a specific chapter to give you enlightening knowledge on how to locate those coins.

We will not be discussing how to decide on the worth or how to understand a coin's significance, as we have discussed all of that in the prior chapters. In this section, we will be talking about all possible ways and places you can explore for collecting or locating coins.

4.1 Where to Locate the Coins

Here are the options you should look up to.

4.1.1. Coin shops

The first most spot you will hit while searching for coins worth collecting is the coin shops. With coin collection being a trend now, there will be various coin shops around your city. You need to run your bit of the research to determine which shops have genuine coins and are pricing them reasonably.

Talk to some of your coin collector friends and discuss which coin shops are better than the rest for starting off with your collection. Visit them all and take a quotation on the coins that you want to purchase. Compare the pricing, quality, genuineness and all of the other aspects before finalizing on one.

Remember, a poor-quality coin might be priced lower than a good-quality coin. It is true that both coins are of the same value, but the quality of their appeal will help you get a higher value in the long run. So, don't get carried away with just affordability in mind, but consider other quality aspects as well.

Make a good bond with the coin shop owners, and instruct them to get in touch with you whenever they get the coin you asked for. Sometimes, a rare collectible coin arrives and gets sold in a flash. And if you are on good terms with the coin shop owner, they will hold it, especially for you. With this, you will be getting a good price for your coins, and you don't have to worry about wandering across various platforms or portals to acquire rare ones.

4.1.2. Coin Shows

The next big platform for you to locate your rare collectible coins is the coin shows. You need to keep in mind that coin shows are more like auctions, where more and more people will be willing to pay a hefty amount for a rare collectible coin. So, you need to be the first in order to reduce the competition and get your set of coins.

The coin shows are most popular across various countries in the world. People from all parts of the world come to attend renowned and famous coin shows to fulfill their craving for rare coins. If you have a series and a set of coins in mind for a purchase, you might possibly find them in such big coin shows.

If you know any of the organizers or hosts, then you can take a confirmation of the coin's availability before traveling all the way to the show. If you are a complete beginner, then there are a few things you should know before attending your first coin show. We shall discuss the same next.

Firstly, you shouldn't be afraid of asking questions to anyone out there. Being a coin collector demands you to earn numismatic knowledge. Therefore, at every table, you visit, keep on asking questions. For instance, ask them about what they are selling and what their specialty is. Talk to them about their most popular items and how they price them. Most of the coin dealers who have set up their tables in the show will be more than happy to answer your questions.

It is because a dealer or a collector knows that an inquisitive collector who asks questions can eventually be a paying customer. If you have a specific taste in a coin series or genre, ask questions about it, and check the availability as well.

Secondly, you should try and visit as many tables as possible. Don't settle for the first offer you get in a coin show. You might find a better deal in the further tables. Even if not for buying, you should still consider visiting almost all tables to ensure you get to know more about coins, how it was bought, how rare is it and how effective they will it be if you trade them.

Remember, this is just like building a relationship with a coin shop owner. If you can get along with them for the long term, then you might be able to source the necessary rare coins right over a call. These dealers who run the shows have a great network and can make the necessary arrangements to get you the coin you need. The pricing might vary, depending on how and from whom they source the coins, but you will eventually get your deal.

So, make sure you explore the entire floor before you decide on whom to rely on for your coin purchase. Thirdly, the most important thing is to maintain etiquette. You don't want people to interrupt you or the dealer while you are in conversation with him/her. Similarly, you shouldn't be in that position either. If you see a dealer engaged in communication with another customer, move on to the next table, and you can come back later to them when they are free to attend to the next customer.

You need to know that the negotiation window in the coin collection arena is very narrow. You need to be strategic in your negotiations but always allow the dealer to make some profit out of their sales. It is a start of a good relationship in this field. Dealers often bring their best pieces to the shows, so don't consider negotiating if you think the price is fair. It is because only reputed dealers are allowed to set up tables in a show, and they undergo serious background checks to ensure they don't sell out fake coins.

One big problem that mostly happens in all of the coin shows is shoplifting. Dealers lose a lot of money and coins due to shoplifting in these shows. So, to ensure that your posture and way of approach towards the dealer don't look suspicious, make sure you do not keep your bag or purse on your lap or on the floor between the legs.

Buying coins for your collection and learning about numismatics go hand in hand. So, make sure you do it while you are in the show. If you are just silently exploring the floor, you might get a few coins in exchange for money, but you won't be learning anything new about the rare coins that exist in the market.

4.1.3. Online Community

There are several coin communities available online that have hundreds of members who have been in this field for a long time now. In some of the communities, you will also find professional numismatists who share their insight into some of the rarest coins. In this community, you will find some of the coin dealers and collectors putting their verbal or textual ads for selling a series or set of coins.

If you are an updated member of the community, then you will have the opportunity to bid for the coins that are listed for sale over it. It is now upon the seller to pick the best deal from the list and sell it off. You don't have to bid for all the coins that are put up for sale over the online community. Instead, you should save your money and bidding capabilities for only the coins that you actually want in your collection.

Moreover, this online community is going to help you sell off some or all of your collection in the future as well. So, it's better to stay active on one or more online communities that are based on coin collection and knowledge. You can also make personal interactions with people you want from the community. Get to know them better and understand their level of expertise in coin collection.

If you are a beginner, then you can find a great mentor from these online communities who will help you with more rare coins through their network.

4.1.4. Mail Order and Website

There are websites and platforms that allow you to place your online orders for select coins. All you have to do is find the trusted platforms and check out their policies on trading or selling coins. Some of the platforms will allow you to directly place your orders through the given porta, whereas some will demand you to place a mail order.

Mail order is nothing but a traditional way of requesting goods from a dealer or service provider. In terms of buying coins, you will be doing the same by mentioning the series of coins you want to buy, the quantity and other associated details and posting it to the company's address. Such companies that accept mail orders will provide you with a catalog of their current inventory.

You need to list the code they associated with each coin or series of coins and mention the quantity according to their stock. They will process the same and keep you updated on the progress of the delivery.

But, as the world is adapting to digital means of availing services and products, the websites are accountable to be more convenient in terms of placing orders for select coins. On the website, you will have a digital catalog of all available coins. It's just like ordering your groceries, fashion accessories or other such shopping goods from various online platforms.

You pick the coins, add them to the cart, add the delivery address, make the payment, and your shipment will be dispatched. Your set of coins will be at your doorstep within the estimated time specified by the dealer website.

4.1.5. The market of all Kinds or Flea Markets

The best thing about collecting coins is their rising popularity. It doesn't matter if you are keen on collecting ancient gold or silver coins, or the ones that are minted a few decades back, you will get them all in local flea markets of specific cities and towns as well.

The only demerit of buying from flea markets is that beginners might not be able to distinguish between the original and fake sellers. Flea markets give you moderately rare coins at a very good price because even a little profit is justified for them. But, to ensure you don't get fooled by the scammers here at flea markets, make sure you take an experienced coin collection friend with you.

Thus, this is the time when your networking and bonding skills will come to work. In all the methods specified above, we constantly guided you to make good bonds with dealers and other coin collectors. Well, now is the time you can use that friendship to get some genuine coins at affordable bucks. Coin flea markets are famous across various countries in the world. So, try your luck to find the desirable coins here as well.

4.1.6. Auctions

One of the best places to get guaranteed rare and priceless coins are auctions. There are both online as well as offline auctions for collectible coins. Some people often want to sell off their entire collection of coins that they gathered throughout their life. It is often done when the person needs money or is now satisfied or done with collecting coins.

In such cases, they hand over the responsibility of auctioning the coins to a third-party company. They hold an auction at a venue and invite all known and reputable coin collectors. They set a minimum bidding amount for all the coins and started the auction process for each of them.

You can take part in one or more of these auctions to bid for the coins that you feel worthy or need. Bid strategically to ensure that you don't pay too much price for a coin that's not worth the amount.

Apart from that, you can also take part in online auction sites. Online auction sites, such as eBay, allow collectors to place bids over the minimum set amount for specific coins. The coin collectors directly upload their collection over the sites and enable people to bid for it. At the end of the bidding period, the highest bidder will get the coin upon processing the payment.

Look out for such options online on eBay or other such platforms and place your bids for acquiring the coin you want. The strategy remains the same as that of the physical auction. You need to bid only the amount that you think is legit for a coin. If you want any of it badly, then you might have to cross the maximum specified bidding limit as per your calculation to acquire it. It totally depends on how far you want to go to bring in a rare collectible coin to your collection.

Apart from such sites, there are some third-party online auctioning websites as well that take up people's collections on contract for selling it off their website. When sold, they will charge a percentage of commission for providing them with the facility. But, as you are locating the coins, this commission is not something for you to consider. You can research some of those sites and try your luck in locating your desired set of rare coins.

4.1.7. Other Coin Collectors

The last way to acquire coins from the market to your collection is by approaching other coin collectors directly. If you don't want any mediators to get involved and charge commissions, you can directly connect with reputed collectors and visit them to pitch your needs. If they are in good intentions to sell their collection to you at a price, you might be open to negotiation.

When you first meet the other collectors, make sure you get an understanding of what they own and what their passion is for coin collection. If they have been collecting coins as an investment, they might quote you the price accordingly. But, if it's just a hobby, you might have a good negotiation window with them. So, you need to study the collectors and their passion for this coin-collecting profession before you can extend your offer.

In most cases, the coin collectors would like to trade and build a relationship with more of their kind. Hence, they will mostly agree on trading. Find a list of coin collectors from your city or locate them based on the type of collection they own. Most coin collectors have social media handles today. You can just check out information about the collection they own and fix an appointment for a meetup.

Keep taking follow-ups with them to arrange a meeting, following which you can extend your pitch towards buying one of their coins or a whole series that they own.

4.2 How to Buy Coins

4.2.1. How to Buy Coin Online

Among all the feasible ways of getting the coins for collection, online buying is something that adds convenience to most of the new and existing collectors. It is because searching and exploring coins online is not at all a strenuous job, and one can source coins from all over the world without any geographical boundaries. Therefore, it's important to get an insight into how one can buy coins online.

As discussed earlier, one can either join an online community, club, or organization, take part in coin auctions online or buy from the coin marketplaces with fixed rates. Let's help you out with the steps you got to follow for each of these online coin-collecting methods:

4.2.2. How to Participate in Online Coin Auctions

There are various websites out there that either sell the listed coins at a fixed price or put up an auction for people to bid. One such example is eBay. You get to bid on the price set by the dealer or collector over the platform, following which the highest bidder at the end of an auction will get that coin.

You don't have to do much to take part in such auctions. The only steps you have to follow are:

- Register yourself over the auctioning website. May it be eBay or any other known coin auctioning platform.
- Fill in your details as a bidder and enter some of the personal details as asked.
- Once done, you will get a catalogue of coins available on the site, with the ones that are active for bidding.

- You can also search for the type of coins you are looking to avail of or search through the specified categories over the platform.
- Once you find the coin you want to bid for, you will see the minimum price set for the coin and the current bidding amount listed right underneath it.
- You must bid above it to take part in the auction of that coin.
- Remember that, in most cases, the auction duration for a coin is very short. So, you might have to be on the bidding screen to cross-bid for the amount that has been surpassed by other bidders to win it.
- If you give the winning bid, then you will be notified with the redirecting payment page, where you must select your preferred payment method. Once the payment is made, the coin or series of coins will be shipped to your given address.

4.2.3. How to Find and Join Coin Collection Club and Organizations

Search for coin-collecting clubs and organizations over social media platforms. You will find a lot of open clubs, groups or community that welcomes collectors for discussions and trading. Join one or more of them to get started with your coin-buying journey.

You can also find dedicated online communities by running a Google search. Get inside and see the kind of interactions and discussions that the members are indulged in. You will get a lot to learn and a chance to buy a lot of collectible coins at the best rates, quoted directly by the collectors, without any mediators.

Professional numismatists in the club or community will also be sharing insights into how worthy a particular coin is. So, whenever a coin is put up for sale in these communities, you can consult the numismatists in the group to give their advice on the quality and worth for you to decide if you should go for it.

4.2.4. Coin Collection Process

You are now aware of how to locate your coins from various sources. Now, it's time for you to direct your attention toward starting off with the collection process. If you don't know the right coin collection process, you will eventually not be enjoying this profession and won't be reaping many benefits from it.

The first set of purchases you make is often rash collections. Once you know how to locate them, you can just head out and buy the first set of coins that you think are precious to you. Based upon immediate or limited knowledge, your preference for coins won't be judged. But make sure you get the set assessed by some knowledgeable coin collector or dealer. It will help you get an idea of what is precious in your existing collection and what's not.

Considering your first purchase as a rash collection, you can just sell off the ones that won't add value to your passion, hobby, or investment. Now, as it's often said, never to make the same mistakes again, you should probably follow a roadmap to implement the right coin collection process, the next time you head out to locate them in the above-mentioned sites.

It is often expected for new collectors to try and jump into the field quickly. They just want to complete their sets and flaunt their collection. But remember that the best coin collectors who possess the most valuable and priceless set of coins have done it over the course of time. Patience is a virtue, not just in the coin-collecting arena but in every aspect of life.

It's literally impossible for anyone to purchase all the great coins within a short period of time. Great coins are often rare and can possibly be found almost anywhere around the world. So, if you can source them all within a short course of time, then you are either buying the fake ones or buying the ones with poor quality and no long-term value at all.

As a new coin collector, you should avoid the temptation after your first purchase. This is why you should connect with an experienced collector or a trusted dealer to help you understand the genuineness of your first collection. From the next, there should be no impetuous decisions from your end upon buying any random coin that has a resemblance to the one that you always wanted. Wait, judge, and then decide!

You don't want to keep buying coins that have no value in the market. If you are collecting them as a scope of investment, then such ravish purchases will not give you any return later in life. Anyone who approaches coin collection or numismatics with a wrong attitude will certainly lose a lot of money. But at the same time, the happy statistic is that most pure collectors make money, it is because they learn to carefully research all of the coins that interest them before making the purchase.

We want you to get the right value for every coin that you purchase by learning the right collection process. And, as this eBook intends to guide you on the pathway of being a successful coin collector, this section is all about educating you on the steps you should follow to get started with the rightful coin collection process.

When you have the right steps in hand, it will be easy to ensure that you don't repeat the same mistake of buying an inappropriate or unworthy coin for your collection. Follow all of these steps completely to win as a coin collector and earn more in terms of profitable investment.

The steps are as follows:

- **Start to Gather Coins**

As stated earlier, the first step is to get the necessary education on various priceless coins and decide on the ones that interest you. Now that you have the right source to locate the coins get along with all the options and try and find the ones that you need. Sooner or later, you will get the series of coins you always desired to add to your collection.

But are they all genuine? Do you know the right way of judging their quality, value, and other such aspects? If not, then consider taking a professional along with you to judge the same on the spot. In this way, you would be spending unwanted money on coins that will lose value over time.

Suppose you like a coin from the series, which you need to complete your set. But the one available at a coin event is rusted, has chipped edges, and the stampings over it are fading away. In that case, if you rush and buy it just for the sake of completing your collection, you will end up losing your scope of earning profit out of it in the long run. The price you pay for buying it now can't be recovered at the time you sell it in the long run.

If there's a chance of buying the same coin with good quality, then no reputed or rich collector would like to spend their money on buying a rusted one. Thus, you will be at a loss.

So, even if you don't trust someone or have no collector colleagues, you can think of it yourself. It is the basic rule of buying and collecting coins! By using just this basic rule and by implementing your other associated coin collection knowledge, you will be able to gather a lot of quality coins that will reap profitable perks in the long run.

Even if you buy a non-precious coin, but it is of good quality, then you can sell it off to the coin dealers for a considerable amount when you head out for validation of value. As a beginner, no one expects you to be proficient with the value of all coins that you own. So, you need a trusted partner to help you with it.

Despite the way you get started with a coin collection, make sure you have enough quality coins that hold value in the market. With this, your first step of gathering the coins is done.

- **Coin Collecting Techniques**

In association with the previous step, you can improve your quest to collect coins by implementing five brilliant techniques. As of now, you are aware of where to look for coins and how to gather them by assessing the basic standards of quality. But, with these techniques, you will level up from being an amateur to a specialist in collecting coins.

The techniques are as follows:

- *Don't Go with the First Option*

When you see the coin you like being displayed in an auction, coin event or an online website, you can't control your temptation. Isn't it? But you ought to hold onto it with patience. We talked about it a little earlier in this section! Being patient is the key to getting the best version of that coin, which might be placed right on the next table in a coin event.

But, if you have just spent your money to cater to your temptation by buying the coin at the first table you saw it, you will then regret it when you see a better one on the next table. Considering you are a beginner; you won't find it feasible to spend a whole lot of money to avail of the better coin as well. And, the previous dealer won't take the coin back, considering you have a mindset of buying it from someone else. So, you are just stuck with your investment for a long time.

To ensure this doesn't happen, make sure you hold onto your temptation. If you fear that someone else might just take that coin, by the time you explore the whole website, coin event or auction collections, then that won't be much of a concern. But if you see a good quality coin after making a purchase from the first store, the regret and loss would be unmatched.

So, always expect the worst in the field of coin collection, and you will never feel disappointed. In this way, when you finally get the perfect set of coins, you will eventually reap the benefits of it.

- _Buy a Book_

There are some reputed books out there with a list of coins with their current or ranged price value. Make sure you go through it before you make further coin purchases. It will help you identify the exact coins that you need to satisfy your purpose.

There are different collectible coins that either satisfy your passion or fulfil your need for investment. So, judge those aspects by referring to the popular coin collection books.

- *Catalogue the Collection*

It's important for you to catalogue your coin collection to ensure you easily stay updated with what you own and what you don't. Don't store it in a scattered manner, as you might just lose track of what series is complete and what isn't. It is evident that you won't remember what coins you already have and what you don't by heart.

So, without cataloguing, there is a possibility you might end up buying repetitive coins and block your investment. So, make sure you catalogue the collection. Apart from helping you win over a good coin collection; cataloguing will also help the next generations to identify the coins and their proper placements when you are not around anymore.

In this way, they will be able to carry your legacy forward by continuing with a coin collection or by completing the incomplete series you left behind.

- *Identify a Particular Theme*

The next technique is to identify a theme that will be more enjoyable for you to collect. For instance, you can consider all coins from the 18th century or all coins that have a specific imprint on them. Depending on the theme, you can direct your search for coins and make the journey more intriguing.

Irrespective of whether you enjoy American history or just want to collect coins that were minted in foreign nations, picking a theme makes it easier to decide. You will have a reputation in the market for the theme you choose. People will remember you as a collector who has a destined focus on collecting coins from specific nationalities.

Following that, more and more people with an interest in the same theme will be lured to present you with an offer to buy one or more coins from your collection. You are free to set your charges and earn profit.

4.2.5. Learning from another Dealer

It is the easiest and most obvious step that you can follow. Make friends with a coin dealer, and make sure you are dealing with him/her over time. Take enough time and ensure that you build a good bond with the dealer. They have a very wide network and are friends with many coin collectors. So, you need to build a bond to ensure that you can trust him/her with your coins and any suggestion they give you.

Take their suggestions on how you can improve your coin collection. Tell them about your current strategies and ask them if there's anything to amend in the approach. Being a dealer and collector, they will guide you with the right strategies on when to hit the market and when to put your money. Don't just follow their suggestions blindly. Instead, take your time to analyse the perks and possible flaws. Get along with the process, and you will eventually have better sets in your collection.

4.2.6. Decide what to Omit

In the last step of your coin collection process, you should finally be ready to let go of some of the coins from your collection. If you don't have endless money to spare for your coin collection, then the best way to acquire more precious coins is to keep rotating. The coins that are of not much value can be traded for the ones that will help you earn big bucks in the long run.

So, take the help of a professional, a book or talk to an expert coin collector to decide which coins you should omit. Use the money you get from it to buy more coins to satisfy your motive. So, these are the steps you should follow to be right in your approach to collecting coins from varying sources. Explore all your options before you decide on buying one. In this way, you will end up making more money out of your coin-collecting profession. Even if you are doing it just as your hobby, having priceless and quality coins is what will give you the reputation of an astounding coin collector.

Volume 5
Types of Coins and their Value

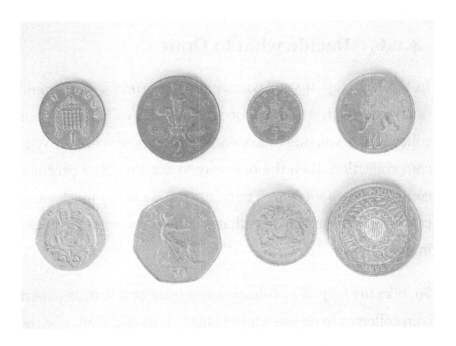

The craze of coin collection increased astoundingly in the 19th century. There were many beginner collectors who started with their coin collection enthusiasm. Just like coin collection as a hobby, passion, or investment are demanding quest for people, rare types of coins are also of utmost importance. Not all collectors are aware of all types of coins and collectible items that they can add to their overall collection.

In the 20th century, the coin-collecting fraternity finally picked up the pace, and people started to know about bullion coins, art bars, pennies, silver certificates, etc. Apart from just coins, there are a lot more valuable items for you to collect. So, it's important for all collectors to get a clear insight into these types of coins and collectible items to ensure the journey becomes more fruitful in the long run.

So far in the book, you have already developed your knowledge and awareness of how to become a coin collector and get started with collecting them from various sources. We have talked about finding information about rare and collectible coins in books from dealers, experienced collectors, and other such information resources.

But, before you head out to those books, you need to understand how the numismatics world categorizes the various series of coins. All the coins are specifically categorized for collectors to find it convenient to understand the value and importance of each coin. Numismatists do research on the coins and categorize them under specific options.

5.1 Types of Coins

To help prepare you for stepping into the coin collection or numismatic world, let's clearly discuss all available categories of coins that you can collect or research.

5.1.1. Ancient Coins

For all historians and archaeologists, ancient coins are considered chronological markets. These coins are not responsible for contributing to the economy, scientific, or political developments. The ancient coins add value to the coin collecting aspects because we know that coins have been used for trading goods and services for more than 3000 years now.

These ancient coins are stated as miniature artworks, and the analytical chemistry behind them is what explains their tones and colors of them. The first batch of metal coins appeared back in 700 BC in the Middle East. They were made of gold and silver. These were the metals that were mostly used by the ancient inhabitants for trading goods and services. These were the only two metals that were accessible to people back then.

In the ancient era, people were unaware of the technology and chemistry of extracting metal from binary compounds.

Therefore, they used to stamp the coins with hand-made molds to create a valuable impression of the ruling king, to mark the specific batch of coins belonging to an individual kingdom.

Due to this chemical inactivity in ancient coins, the gold and silver appeal stays intact even after centuries of being exposed to the atmosphere or buried underground. Moreover, when buried, these coins also experience interaction with corrosive chemicals, which has deteriorating capabilities for the coins that are made today. But gold and silver used back then were discovered in brilliant condition. Thus, the worth of such coins increases among coin collectors and numismatists.

Later, as the usage of the coin became more popular in ancient times, gold and silver coins were stated as trading currency of the highest value. But to expand the currency system, ancient people introduced copper, brass, bronze, and electrum coins as well. Thus, it became easier for people to trade more conveniently.

All the ancient coins did vary in terms of design, importance, and quality. Most of them were preferably used by everyday people, while some of the coins were used specifically by kings and emperors in the past. There are many types of ancient coins that were discovered in the modern era, but only a few of them became enduring pieces in terms of historical richness.

The ancient coins are categorized as important and have great value because they commemorate some of the crucial historical events or moments, representing western civilization. Apart from that, some of the ancient coins also represent the highest form of artistic works. Such coins weren't minted or made ever again, for 2000 years. Only a handful of ancient coins survive today in the hands of several collectors, in museums or with numismatists.

The Brutus "Eid Mar" Denarius, 42 BC, is one of the most important and demanding ancient coins of all. It marks one of the most important events in the history of western civilization, which was Julius Caesar's assassination. In this ancient coin, you will find a portrait imprint of Brutus on one side and a pileus or cap of liberty on the other side, with the impression of two daggers.

The daggers are referred to as the pugio and were probably representing the weapons that were used for killing Julius Caesar. One of these daggers represents Brutus, whereas the other represents Cassius, who conspired in the assassination with Brutus. The pileus made over the coin refers to the cap that was given to slaves as a tradition for freedom.

This coin states that Brutus, along with Cassius, assassinated Julius to liberate the Republic from the reign of a dictator.

So, this is how ancient coins represent a significance to historical events or moments, which is what adds value to them with respect to the coin collector's perspective.

5.1.2. Modern Coins

The craze of coin collection increased during the 19th century. During this period, some novice collectors came to the scene. They started showing their interest in collecting not just ancient coins but also modern coins across the world that were minted and stopped being circulated in the past.

As stated earlier, the coins worthy to be collected are categorized as chronological markers. Therefore, collectible coins are distinguished based on two chronological categories. All the coins that were minted or made for use on or before 1964 are considered vintage or ancient coins. At the same time, all the coins that were made on or after 1965 are termed modern coins.

There are many other differences between these two categories of coins, apart from just the dates. All the modern coins get graded, valued, collected and traded in a very distinct manner from that of the ancient coins. All the modern coins that are available for collectors are often available in high grades. The coins that were released for circulation in the modern era are quite easy to locate or source.

Apart from that, the non-circulating coins such as proof coins, bullion issue eagle coins and others, were most likely graded even higher and had a higher value too. A small percentage of all the modern coins were also designated as PR 70 or MS 70. In some cases, all the 70-graded modern coins cost a heavy premium for collectors to buy them.

It means that the look of the coin with grades 69 and 70 might not be much different, but the value differs dramatically. An Eisenhower dollar is considered an unusual coin and is very rarely seen to be circulated. But the collector value of it is very small. Just like that, a proof gold buffalo coin of 2006 might seem beautiful and has a presentable appeal, but the worth of it sticks to just 10 to 20% on the melt.

The collectors need to be very careful while they are trading modern coins, as it's easy for rookies to end up overpaying for a low-valued coin. Modern coins represent brilliant value in terms of long-term hikes in their worth. Most numismatists state modern coins as being inferior in terms of collector value when compared to that vintage or ancient coins.

It is because numismatists believe that there are plentiful coins of specific modern categories, available in the market. Thus, they also lack any important historical significance. With such an argument being made, numismatists believed that the value of these modern coins would not appreciate immensely over time. But, with further research and the rising demand for modern coins among coin collectors, it was again stated that modern coins might just be an emerging category that has immense potential in terms of adding value to numismatics and coin collection aspects.

It was noted that a traditional coin collector preferred collecting silver eagles or other such coins by date and other parameters. People took it as fun and enjoyment, as collecting such modern coins is affordable in comparison to buying their ancient counterparts. Moreover, completing the coin sets was easy with modern coins.

But there were certain modern coins, such as gold eagles, that were scarce and of very high value. Such coins that were minted with low quantities and were circulated only for a minimum time, with the representation of great achievements or moments of respective countries, have the highest of values in the modern numismatic world. Over time, the modern coins or issues were considered fewer bullion items and more true collectible coins.

Apart from this understanding, you must also know that modern coins are different from ancient coins in terms of pricing, rarity, and condition. Every collector works towards their specific preferences. The quality of a coin that seems unappealing to one buyer might seem attractive to the other. Hence, when you buy modern coins at good price levels, they will give you great value in the long run as collectibles or bullion products.

5.1.3.   Gold & Silver or Bullion Coins

Gold and silver coins are also stated as bullion coins. Basically, bullion coins are made out of precious materials, and gold & silver are the prime metals that make a coin fall under this category. Most countries have their official set of bullion coins.

For instance, you can consider the American Eagle series of gold and silver coins produced by the US mint and the Canadian Maple Leaf set of bullion coins made by the Royal Canadian Mint. These physical coins are made out of gold and silver, but some bullion coins are made up of even precious metals, including palladium or platinum.

Most investors buy gold and silver bullion coins as collectible items. The value of these coins will increase in the forthcoming time because of the rising inflation across the world. So, if you are collecting coins in the form of an investment, then this category is quite perfect for you to start with. It does need a higher investment at the start but will end up giving you a very profitable value.

Gold and silver coins have been existing among us for more than a thousand years now. They were used as primary currencies throughout various historical evidence. But, when the modern-day fiat currency system was introduced, these bullion coins were then regulated and considered as an investment or collectible item for people.

The collectors buy these gold and silver or bullion coins, based on their aesthetic beauty and rarity. These two factors play a major role in increasing the base value of these coins. The value that is specified for the metals used in making these coins are considered as melt value, whereas the demand, beauty or rarity is considered as the numismatic value.

As a coin collector or investor, you can expect to have an edge against rising inflation when you buy such gold and silver coins. Most of the coin collectors who own these bullion coins are quite unhappy with how the fiat currency system is failing drastically in terms of preventing poor government policies. Therefore, gold and silver coins are often considered best for coin collection as an investment.

To help you understand the worth of such bullion coins, let's give you a brief insight into the American Eagle coin. American Eagle is a series of gold coins that is one of the most popular bullion coins across the globe. These coins are minted with 22-karat gold that has 91.67% purity. These coins are also available in four different weights, which include 1/10th, 1/4th, ½ and one troy ounce.

Imagine the worth of gold with such high purity being stamped in the form of coins. Some of the other demanding gold and silver or bullion coins that collectors should consider buying are Chinese Gold Pandas and South African Krugerrands. They are easy to source but difficult to buy because the pricing doesn't fit the budget of all coin collectors. Therefore, you might have to start slowing with affordable coin sets, before you can head out to buy gold and silver or bullion coins.

5.1.4. Commemorative Coins

The commemorative coins are issued by the mints of the respective government for celebrating any specific national event that holds utmost importance. In most the cases, the celebration occasions include any royal wedding, diamond jubilee, and others. These coins are very rarely found in usual circulation around the countries. Moreover, such coins are also sold to people as souvenirs.

All the commemorative coins are very much popular among coin collectors from across the world. Irrespective of which mint issued specific sets of commemorative coins, they will always fall under one of these three types:

- Everyday Commemorative Currency

The regularly used coins with specific value have commemorative stamps to make them significant and celebration-worthy. These coins are usually made of base metals and not precious ones. Such coins are minted in a very less quantities and are circulated with usual means among the people of the country.

- Non-Circulating Commemorative Legal Tender Coins

It is the category of older coins such as Crowns, Sovereigns or modern 5 Euro coins of the UK, and equally value coins from other parts of the world that were either made up of precious or base metals. As per government policies, these coins can be circulated depending on individual preferences. But they don't get circulated so often because of their definite spot or collectible value.

The collectible value of these non-circulating commemorative coins is very high than that of the issuing price of their legal tender.

- Souvenir Commemorative Tokens

The commemorative proof issues being minted with gold or silver, which are not legal tenders, are considered commemorative souvenir tokens. Such coins are available in limited numbers, for which the collectors look out for them at a demanding rate.

Remember, all the commemorative or usual circulation coins that are minted by the authorities are considered legal tender. But that doesn't intend that the usual and commemorative coins share the same value. No shops, businesses or banks accept commemorative coins for cash transactions if they are specified as collectibles or are made of precious metals.

There is a specific category termed circulating legal tender issues, which can be traded or spent with businesses, banks, and shops. Thus, you can conclude that commemorative coins are one of the best collectible assets for coin collectors and numismatists. Getting your hands on rare commemorative coins will get you higher worth than that their face value while it was minted.

The value of a commemorative coin is calculated by referring to the condition, mintage year, minting errors, mint mark, and recent bullion value. As per experts, both everyday, as well as celebration commemorative coins are of great value. The everyday coins will quickly gain value when the item lacks availability in circulation due to unavoidable wastage.

5.1.5. Revolutionary Coins

The revolutionary coins are historical collectibles that have the impressions of incredible accomplishments acquired by important personalities. Such coins can add a very high value to your overall coin collection. The American revolution coins are great examples of the highest significance, which began being issued in the year 1775. These coins had the artistic impression of all important personalities who fought for the United States.

Some of the American revolutionary coins include Two Bits, Spanish Piece of Eight, Continental Dollar, Massachusetts Pine Tree and many more. Most countries with rich histories have dedicated revolutionary coins and are circulating them as souvenirs. They have a high value and good demand among collectors.

The revolutionary coins have the same importance as the commemorative coins. It is because, just like commemorative issues showcase recent celebrations, revolutionary coins showcase past achievements and accomplishments.

5.1.6. Souvenir Pennies

The pressed pennies are made by the process of stretching, flattening, and printing. Each of these pennies has a unique design, which is mostly preferred as souvenir tokens. These pressed pennies have been in the market for more than a century now. Earlier, these pennies were made by placing the metals on railway tracks for trains to press them to optimal measures. Earlier, the designs were hand-crafted, which adds value to them for modern collectors.

All the souvenir pennies that were made before 1982 are considered by coin collectors, as the value significance is higher. Before 1982, these coins were made out of copper, which has a value among collectors of today. After the era, there were reports on the use of zinc for the making of these pressed pennies, which leaves silver marks over them, that don't add to the value significance at all.

The pressed or souvenir pennies first appeared back in 1892 at the World's Columbian Exposition, which was a yearlong program for celebrating the 400th anniversary of Christopher Columbus's arrival in America. Back in that time, there were four designs for people to choose from for getting their pressed souvenir tokens. Thus, it is the first recorded instance of souvenir tokens, but there is a possibility that pressed pennies were made even before that, with the use of train tracks.

As coin collectors, you need to look for souvenir tokens that date back to the old times. Today, there are many machines out there at various tourist spots that help people get souvenir tokens for themselves at ease. But these tokens are not worth collecting for a collector who wants value hidden behind every coin he/she possesses. Go to the coin shows or talk to dealers about sourcing souvenir tokens that date before 1982.

5.1.7. Medallions

Just like the pressed pennies, a medallion is an artistic object, that represents the appeal of a coin. It is a thin disc that is made of metal and has a design on both sides. The purpose of making these medallions is to showcase some form of celebration or awards. For coin collectors, you should know that the medallions are only worthy to be collected if they haven't been used as a medal.

As medallions are also souvenirs, they are specifically designed for events, celebrations, or places such as museums, heritage sites, fairs, expositions and others. The medals that represent royal connections or military honors are of high value and rarely available in the coin collection market. Apart from that, the educational rewards, sports prizes or religious artifacts of the past also add value to the medallion collection.

Politicians have showcased a great impact on giving this world some great historical events for shaping the respective countries. Therefore, there have been several medals made and preserved to reflect all of those events. Such medallions link back the country to its history and give a brief explanation of the achievements, motivations, and appearances.

Coronations, births, deaths and jubilees were also stamped in the form of commemorative medallions for special occasions. It is to honor the respective person or occasion. Such medallions were given alongside other souvenir goods. They acted as a reminder to families that held power in the past or will describe important unions.

Such medallions of the past are considered great investment opportunities for coin collectors. Depending on the worldly significance in portrays, the value of it will be very high at the time you sell it off to other collectors.

5.1.8. Error Coins

Error coin, as the name suggests is the type of coin that wasn't properly made during the minting process. While the coins are being manufactured in the mint, there's a possibility of any visible error being detected in a batch. Some problems that lead the coins to be considered as error coins are wrong planchet, improper production of planchets, center being struck off, too thin, too thick or others.

Such scenarios conclude that a coin or a batch of coins is full of errors. Thus, they don't get approved for circulation. The errors are mostly linked to dying, planchet or strikes. These coins are also called mint errors, which is now adding uniqueness and excitement among coin collectors to acquire them all under their collection.

The different types of mint errors are as follows.

- **Die Cap Error:** Such a mint error occurs in a coin when a new planchet is placed onto the coin press without ejecting the previous one. Thus, the first planchet will stick to the coin dyes. When repeated strikes are made, the first planchet will then take the shape of the bottle cap. Thus, a batch of error coins is made.

- **Use of Wrong Planchet:** At times, people who make coins at the mint might use the wrong planchet in the coin press. Thus, the planchet doesn't match the dyes that are present within the press. As a result, incorrect coins are stamped.

- **Off-Center Errors:** Such an error occurs when the planchet is not properly centered between the dyes within a coin press.

- **Partial Collar Errors:** Here, the coining collar is only partially connected to the press, which results in inappropriate edges of the coin.

- **Broadstrike Errors:** Coining collar is responsible for holding the coin at the center of both dyes. In this error case, the collar isn't engaged properly, but the coin still gets repetitive strikes.

- **Double and Triple Strike Error:** It is a very common error that mostly happens when a coin is struck more than once to determine its proper shape. For most times, multiple strikes result in damaged coin impressions.

- **Brockage Errors:** This is a type of error that occurs when one coin is placed over another and is struck within the coining chamber. Thus, the error occurs.

- **Double Denomination Errors:** In this case, one coin is struck first with a specified denomination and is then fed through a coining press, where it was dyed for another denomination.

- **Bonded Coins:** Such an error occurs when two coins get along together while being struck at the coin press.
- **Die Adjustment Error:** It is an error that occurs when the coin gets struck without sufficient pressure when the machine is under any adjustment.
- **Fragment Errors:** When metal fragments from several sources persist within the coin press, they end up being implemented into the coin design. Thus, the coin gets categorized as an error coin.
- **Proof Errors:** The proof coins are meant to be perfectly designed as per the specified standards. Any form of mistake makes it falls under the category of error coins.

But, before you get excited too and get along to buy an error coin, you should know its type and the latest market selling price of it. It is quite difficult for anyone to price the error coins. Therefore, expert guidance is of utmost importance when you are about to buy a series of error coins. At times, the price of a coin solely depends on the rarity, eye appeal, grade, date, and the impact of the striking error.

The price of the error coins also varies depending on the fact when two collectors are bidding for the rare error made by the mint. Use multiple sources to determine the value of a mint error coin. It is because these errors do not fit into one specific category. But, a collector must know that error coins might gain popularity one year and might lose it the next year, as the demand keeps on changing over time.

You can determine the value of an error coin that you own only when you head out to sell it to other collectors or dealers who want it.

5.1.9.   Silver Certificates

The term silver certificate is a dollar bill that represents legal tender but in the form of paper currency. It represented a unique time in the history of America and was issued in the late 1800s by the Federal Government. The holder of silver certificate dollar bills had the liberty of redeeming it in exchange for some amount of silver. It was like an investment for people to own silver without buying the precious metal.

These silver certificate dollar bills do not have any monetary value for being exchanged as silver. But they are still considered legal tender in terms of their face value. Today, silver certificates are considered more worthy than that at face value due to their significance relating back to one of the prospered American decisions. Silver certificates are considered unique artifacts today and hold great value for collectors.

As of today, silver certificates are now obsolete and hold value depending on the condition. So, if you are about to buy silver certificates, make sure you assess the condition and make sure that it can be maintained while in your possession for the long term. Only if you sell it out later in good condition can you ask for a profitable return for your collected certificates.

The silver certificates continued being issued from 1878 to 1964. For one year, from June 1967 to 1968, Americans were allowed to buy silver bullion for themselves in exchange for their silver certificate. After the year 1968, these bills became redeemable only in the form of Federal Reserve bills. Hence, today they are available at an obsolete rate. But these certificates are still legal.

The present value of the silver certificates doesn't depend on their ability to be used as legal tender but in terms of being collected by enthusiasts. The value of these certificates varies depending on the year they were issued, alongside the condition. It is stated that the certificates issued between the years 1935 to 1957 hold high collector value than the other bills.

These bills look very similar to the usual George Washington bills, but with a key difference. The difference is that the silver certificate bill has text that mentions, "One dollar in silver payable to the bearer on demand." Thus, it will be the identification or distinguishing mark for the silver certificates.

Some of the earlier issued silver certificates might just be of great value. For instance, the silver certificate of 1923, with George Washington on the front, as usual, has a very high collector value today. It is because that was the last large-sized format of Washington's portrait on the bills. The silver certificate of 1899 is of added value, which has an eagle on the front, adding uniqueness in comparison to other certificates. Some of the other batches of silver certificates, which featured Martha Washington on the top, are quite valuable and are worth more than $1000 if they are in the best condition.

5.1.10. Art Bars

Art bars are really very popular among investors and collectors. Due to the volatility in the market, coin collectors and investors are now willing to buy precious metals in the form of bullion coins or art bars to strengthen their financial portfolios and protect themselves from price inflation.

Art bars are considered a form of bullions and are a very attractive way of securing investments and adding interesting items to your collection. The art bars have artwork engraved, both on the front and back. Some of the specific art bars also have designs on both of their sides as well. For most times, they were produced to commemorate important historical events, just like the bullion coins.

For instance, you can check the most admired art bar, the United States Bicentennial of 1976. At times, these art bars undergo minting with a very different theme, which can range from being patriotic to displaying four seasons. Some of the special art bar designs in the past have also replicated gorillas, Haley's comet and UFOs.

Art bars are highly fashionable and have high collector value, for you to consider them in your collection. These bars have a very antique feel that adds specific quality to any collection. Therefore, almost all collectors intend to buy a complete set of all art bars to make their collection look vibrant.

Art bars are valuable because some of them have cultural and historical significance. They represent any phenomena that were unique to the respective place or time period. Thus, the value of the market will keep rising in the long run. In comparison to the bullion coins, art bars sell at a higher price than them. It is because the pricing of art bars solely depends on factors such as content, purity, weight, condition, artwork quality and rarity.

The purity, weight and artwork quotient are higher in terms of art bars, which makes them more valuable than the bullion coins. But it is quite tough to determine the exact value of an art bar, as it will depend on what all of the collectors are looking for at the same time. Some of the specific designs are often more popular than others for several reasons. As there are lots of designs out in the market, it is difficult to predict what design would gain or lose demand at what point in time.

Before the times of modern minting, the art bars were made by hand pouring melted metals into the molds, one at a time. It was a very long and tiring process, for which there was less quantity of such art bars. After modern minting was introduced, many art bars were produced at a faster scale. Moreover, the name of the manufacturer was also stamped with a unique serial number.

Most of the designs of the past are timeless and will help you ensure financial security by increasing value in the long run. It ensures delight and enjoyment to the collectors and investors for a long time.

5.2 Understanding the Value of Rare Collectible Foreign Coins

For over centuries, all the foreign nations have been minting coins for circulation. A large quantity of all these coins exists today, that represents minting process, design history and circulation history. The world of foreign coins helps people understand the history and stories associated with the respective country. Therefore, coin collectors from all over the world are curious to collect foreign coins that dates to the historical events or stories.

There are several factors that come into consideration while evaluating the foreign coins. While most of the foreign coins have their respective country's name over it, along with different language impressions. It is quite difficult for people to determine the origin of foreign coins because not all designs deliver the required message to identify the same. As a result, it becomes complex for the collectors to identify which foreign coin holds more value over the others.

Most of the foreign coins that are up for collection today are not accountable to give you any profitable returns. The coins of today are used as per their face values, but the foreign coins that were minted around 100 years ago, are considered as collectible rare items. They are worth a lot of money. Even when you buy them for adding onto your collection, you might have to pay a lot of money to buy just one among the best set of coins.

But, the pricing and the worth of foreign coins is also determined, based on its condition. you must keep in mind that a foreign coin can hold value as a rare collectible or legal tender. For instance, a limited-edition coin that was minted for commemoration, will hold more worth than the usual coins that were minted for circulation.

If you are lucky enough, then you might find a hidden treasure in the form of a foreign coin, in a drawer that your grandfather or great grandfather used back when he was alive. Imaging you are shifting to a new house and found a box full of those coins in a drawer that you never considered cleaning while you lived in that house. You did hit a jackpot with those amazing foreign coins. But you do not know the value of each of them, until you get it examined by someone who knows about coins.

The intention of giving you this example is to help you understand the value of foreign coins that dates back to 100 years or lesser. Owning a bunch of foreign valuable coins is something, but getting the right value against it is another thing. So, whether you get a treasure hidden in your house, or you buy some foreign coins to fulfill your coin collecting urge, you can make profit only when you price them well. If you head out to any usual dealer, without knowing about the market price of coins, you will end up being paid a very minimal amount, which won't do justice to your collection.

Talk to reputed collectors or professional numismatists to determine the value of specific foreign coins that you own or found in your attic. They will guide you with the right pricing, grading, quality, and other such insights associated with your collection. But, if you are an engrossed coin collector, then you already have an idea of certain foreign coins that holds the highest value. There are certain foreign coins that isn't possible to be resting in your attic, as they are very rare.

And such rare coins are the ones that collectors are craving for. You can head out to coin events or auctions, looking out for foreign coins in specific. The ones that are available in abundance are not much of worth in the long run, but you will see people battling or bidding over few specific sets of foreign coins. They are the ones you should target to acquire for your collection. The only way to do that is bid without competition or own it at a higher price than what other collectors are readily offering the dealers or other collectors.

5.2.1. Most important foreign coins in the coin collection market

Here are some of those foreign coins that hold highest importance in the current coin collection market.

- **The Flowing Hair- Silver Dollar of 1794**

The Flowing Hair- Silver Dollar of 1974 sits at the top of rank board in the list of most valuable foreign coins that exists. It is the most expensive foreign coin that has been ever sold to date. Some of the experts even believe that this coin was the first ever silver dollar that was struck by mint of United States.

The frontal features of this coin give an impression of Lady Liberty, whose hair is flowing. The other side of the coin shows an American Eagle, which is also a valuable impression when present in a foreign coin. Only 1800 coins were ever produced, and some of the experts claim that there are only around 120 or 130 of these coins left with the collectors from all over the world. Thus, such an availability makes this coin extremely rare and valuable. Back in 2013, this coin was sold off in an auction, for more than $10 million.

So, if you are to buy this coin and add it to your collection, imagine the money you could make out of it, when the availability of it becomes scarcer in the future.

- **Brasher Doubloon of 1787**

Brasher Doubloon, wase made back in late 18th century, by Ephraim Brasher. He was a silversmith and goldsmith of New York City. He created one of the rarest foreign coins of all time. The frontal features of this coin have an impression of state seal stamped over a rising sun. The other side of the coin has an American Eagle, that is carrying a shield.

The coin is very rare in today's collector market, but there are specific versions of it have different price tags, considering their varying characteristics. In a coin sale event of 2011, a version of Brasher Doubloon was sold for around $7.4 million. This specific coin had an EB signature of Brasher on the bird's breast.

Following that, in a private coin sale of 2018, another Brasher Doubloon with an EB signature on eagle's wing, was sold for more than $ million. A very recent auction of 2021 sold off another Brasher Doubloon, with the highest ever value of $9.36 million. Thus, the value of this coin has already been multiplied exponentially over the course of time. So, if you own one, or are about to add one to your collection, be assured you might make around $10 million out of it at least if you have got the one with right characteristics on it.

- **Fugio Cent of 1787**

Fugio cent of 1787 is not that valuable as the other two specified above, but this cent still is a rare and pricey collectible. There is a very interesting history associated with it. Fugio cent is also recognized as Franklin cent, named after Benjamin Franklin, the founding father. It is a rare collectible, because this might possibly be the first coin ever that was circulated across the US, upon its new formation.

The frontal feature of the coin showcases an impression of sundial and sun, with a motto in Latin that says 'fugio'. The term suggests that the time and sun are flying consistently. At the bottom end of the coin, there is a phrase that says, "Mind Your Business". It is said to have been included in the coin for giving an invocation to bearer for paying attention to the overall business affairs.

The other side of the coin also has a motto that says, "We are One", with an impression of 13 chain links. It is a symbol of formation of the first 13 American states. For new coin collectors, starting off with this foreign coin can be an affordable option to get into this field. You can get a fugio cent coin for just a few hundred dollars. The value of it does increases over time, but not at a very rapid rate as of the other two coins listed above.

Remember, some of the fugio cent coins that are in great condition are also sold for thousands of dollars, with highest recorded amount being $10,000. There are also some rare variants of fugio cent, which might be priced for an even higher amount. So, try and source these coins for a start, and your foreign coin collection quest will begin with the right set.

- ### Lincoln Head Copper Penny Coin of 1943

This is a popular foreign coin that you might find somewhere around your old dresser, or with some popular coin collectors. The conditions that surrounded the country, during the production of these coins is that makes it valuable, rare and interesting. The pennies were minted in US with the use of nickel and copper. But, in those times US needed those materials for war purposes.

Therefore, the mint started using steel as the core material for producing these pennies. But, by mistake there was a batch of these coins that got struck with copper, even after the rules were passed for using steel. This mistake happened because all the blanks were present within the mint, while new steel pennies were made. Thus, these rare copper coins of 1943 with Lincoln's head as the front feature, are extremely rare and valuable.

As per the experts, there are only 40 of these coins remain around the world with collectors or dealers. But some of the numismatists say that there are now less than 20 of them, which makes it even more rare.

There was a verdict by US Mint that says these pennies were very easy to be counterfeited. It is because, it was easy to coat the steel pennies with the use of copper, and the dates were altered to 1943 with certain measures. Counterfeiting of dates was easy for the coins that were made in 1949, 1948 and 1945. But this malpractice didn't last longer, as people used magnets to check the originality of this coin.

The copper version of this coin was sold for more than $204,000 in a coin auction of 2019. One person held onto a specimen of this coin for more than 70 years, after he found it during his school times at the cafeteria. The highest record-selling price of one of the versions of this coin is around $1.75 million, in a coin auction of 2010.

- **Liberty V Nickel of 1913**

It is not as old as most of the other coins in this list but is still one of the most valuable foreign coins you will ever come across. Mint of United States struck this coin from year 1883 to 1913. In the final year, only five reputed coins were minted, to create a vintage effect of this coin in the long run.

Since year 2000, this coin has hit the auctions only a rare times and has been sold for more than millions of dollars. As per a report, one of the versions of this coin was sold for around $4.15 million, in year 2005. Following that, the same coin was again passed on to another collector against an offer of $5 million in year 2007.

Not much later in 2010, another version of this coin came to the auction market and was sold for $3.17 million. The last recorded sale of this coin in 2018 was for a value of $4.56 million.

If you are a new collector, and don't have the budget to get one of these coins in your collection, you can still admire one at some specific museums. One of it is Smithsonian Institution, where these coins are displayed for audience's attention.

- **$1 Million- Canadian Gold Maple Leaf of 2007**

The Canadian Gold Maple Leaf of $1 million was made as a novelty coin. It weighed over 100 kgs, and there were only six of these coins that were ever made by the end of 2022. Each of these coins had a face value of $1 million and were mostly used as a promotional showpiece for the original one-ounce coins of Canadian Gold Maple Leaf series.

The original one-ounce coins are equally rare, and this $1 million coins is now an addition to the demands of this foreign minted coin. The front of this big coin shows the face of Queen Elizabeth II, and the reverse of it has a Canadian maple lead, to represent the series. In an auction of 2010, one of these $1 million coins was sold at around 3.27 million euros or $4 million dollar, as per the conversion of that period.

It is quite rare or next to impossible for any rich coin collector to get one for themselves. But, if you ever come across one, and have the budget to bid on it, don't leave the chance!

- **Various Morgan Silver Dollars**

Morgan silver dollars are not considered rare just by their name, but there are some vintage versions of it, that fetches a very high price at coin auctions and events. The specialty of these coins is its 90% silver composition. The base price for a Morgan dollar is $20, irrespective of the version you own. It is because of silver being used in its making.

But some of the Morgan silver dollars, made in specific years with varying alphabet markings can help you earn more than the base value. Remember to pay attention to the alphabet markings, without which the value will stick to the base amount. Some of those valuable Morgan coins are S Morgan of 1893, Morgan 1901, CC Morgan of 1889, S Morgan of 1884, and O Morgan of 1893.

Each of these specific Morgan dollars can help you get a value ranging between $100,000 to $550,000, depending on the condition. If you are just starting off with coin collection as your hobby, passion, or investment regime, then getting one of the Morgan silver dollars won't be a bad bet. You won't be set back much upon owning them but will eventually become an evident part of country's history through your collection of foreign coins.

- **Pre-1964 American Silver Coins**

Among the cosmos of all foreign coins, one set lies the pre-1964 silver coins of America. Unlike today, the low denomination coins back then were made of pure silver. They have a great value in coin collection market of today. Among all the other coins that's listed here, this set of American pre-1964 silver coins have the highest chance of lying somewhere around the corners of your house or garage. Some of those coins include Mercury dime, Washington quarters and Morgan dollar.

Some of the coins of this era have a rare collectible value, depending on the silver content being used in it, as that of the Morgan dollars. But the other common coins that you own or collect, will have a price hike based on their bullion value. Some of the collectors consider getting these coins, not for their collector value, but for the precious metal used in it.

- **Edward III Florin of 1343**

It is among the world's most expensive foreign coins that was ever made. The Edward III Florin of 1343 is one among the three gold coins that ever existed. Two of the examples are available in London's British Museum, and they were found during excavation of the River Tyne, back in 1857. The third of these coins was found in 2006, with the use of a metal detector, by some prospector.

The frontal feature of this coin has King Edward III, sitting on the throne alongside two leopards. The other side of the coin has a Royal Cross within the quatrefoil. Considering the design, people referred to this coin by the name of, Double Leopard.

As stated earlier, two of these coins are stored in the museum and are probably not for sale. But the third found coin was sold off in an auction for a value of around $850,000, which was a very high value at that period of time, for some British coin. As of today, it is circulating from collector to collector, and an estimated market value of it is around $6.8 million or more. It is extremely difficult for any collector to source and get their hands on this coin.

- **Umayyad Gold Dinar of 723**

Umayyad gold dinar of 7723 is among the most valued foreign coins. It is an Islamic coin and was struck out of gold. The coin consists of a marker that says, "mine of the commander of the faithful". Moreover, it is the first ever Islamic coin that mentioned any location of Saudi Arabia. There are around a few dozens of these foreign coins that exists in the market.

In year 2011, one of these Islamic coins was sold in an auction for around $6 million. It is termed to be as the second-most expensive coin that has been ever sold at any auction. In year 2019, another version of Umayyad gold dinar was sold for around $4.8 million. Thus, it is evident on how precious these Islamic coins are among the coin collectors.

These are all forms of commemorative, bullion and other such foreign coins that have immense value in the modern-day coin collection market. Apart from these reputed names and coin types, there are many other options out there for you to start your collection with. Go for the ones that are moderately available in the coin collection market, for you to get them at a nominal pricing. If there's a commemoration or a history attached to the making of that coin, you should consider holding onto it for a long time.

Over time, when the coin will become scarce in the market, you might just get a whipping value for it, that you purchased for just a mere hundreds or thousands of dollars. The nine options listed above have been ranked as the world's most valuable foreign coins. If you have the budget, and you come across any of them while on your quest of collecting coins, then you can count on giving in your efforts to acquire them.

You can consider starting with some rare European, Mexican, Chinese, and other such coins, before you can count on getting the high valued ones. As a dedicated coin collector, you should spend a lot of your time in just searching for the rare or valuable American coins. But, when searching for foreign coins, there's a need for adding diversity to your collection, for increasing the value of your overall collection. Any foreign coin that has a commemoration or celebration value, is valuable just like the US coins. The prices might not be the same as you expect, but worthy coins of respective countries, are still acceptable to be part of your coin collection. So, look out for options from across the globe.

Volume 6

How to Grade and Evaluate Coins and Detect the Counterfeits

In this book so far, we have discussed about coin grading a several times. Coin collecting beginners must have developed an idea by now that grading determines the quality and condition of coins, which is important in terms of pricing them for sale. There are specific criteria that the numismatists or experts follow to grade the coins.

The criteria consist of many parameters which include strike, color, luster, preservation, country/state and attractiveness.

6.1 How to Grade and Evaluate Coins

Let's see how the coins are graded and evaluated based on these parameters.

6.1.1. Mint State (MS) Grading

Mint State (MS) is responsible for determining the coin's graded condition. It is a designation of the grader for indicating the regular business strike coins, which hasn't been circulated ever. It means, the coins that are in the exact same condition as they were produced at first. Let's see the steps being followed under the MS grading system:

6.1.2. 70-Point Scale Coin Grading

On a 70-point scale of MS coin grading techniques, a coin is graded often between the range of 60 to 70. MS-60 is the grading for a coin that has certain wear marks on it, whereas MS-70 is the grading value for a coin that is flawless in its appeal. MS-70 is the highest grade that any coin can ever achieve, which gets the highest market value.

- **MS-60:** This grading is known was the MS Basal. These coins have ugly marks, no luster and showcases clear contact markings, which degrades its quality and market value.

- **MS-63:** It is known as MS Acceptable. These coins are uncirculated and has some contact nicks and marks. The luster in such coins is slightly impaired, but the appearance is overall appealing. The strike measured on such coins often range from average to weak.

- **MS-65:** This grading is called MS Choice. These coins have strong luster, with minimal contact marks and brilliant new-like appeal. The strike measured for these coins is above average.

- **MS-68:** This grading is called MS Premium Quality. These coins have perfect luster, with no visible marks to naked eyes. The appeal of these coins is outstanding, with sharp & attractive strike.

- **MS-69:** This grading is called MS All-But-Perfect. Here, the coins are with perfect luster, sharp & attractive strike, and elegant appeal. It is next to the perfect coin but has some microscopic flaws which can be viewed only with an 8x magnification. Therefore, such coins are graded as MS-69.

- **MS-70:** This grading is the MS Perfect batch, which is also called as the perfect coin. In these coins, there are no microscopic flaws, even with the 8x magnification. The strike here is real sharp and perfectly at the centers. The strike is made over a perfect planchet, and it gives an outstanding appeal with original luster.

6.1.3. Understanding the Three Bucket for Coin Grading

The three-bucket approach helps the newcomers understand how the coin grading scale is used. Think of using three buckets for the examination, and use first one for circulated, second for About Circulated (AU) and third for MS coins. It is stated as a historical method for the newcomers to grade the coins.

When there was no numismatic understanding about coin grading or coin collection, this three-bucket approach was the only grading system people used to value their coins. In the early 1900s, there was a very small group of people who were keen about coin collection. Therefore, they decided on using only three grades to determine the market value of a coin.

Based on the visual appeal, the coins were put in the three buckets as per the categories specified. Circulated coins with minimal contact marks and retained appeal were added to the first bucket. The AU coins with clear details, shine and good luster was added onto the second bucket. And, the perfect coins with exquisite appeal were added onto the third bucket.

But soon there was a problem in this approach as a lot of coins were being added to the circulated bucket, for which the collectors were losing money on their collectible coins. Therefore, more grading categories were included to this approach, including proof coins. This worked great for the coin collectors, as they were satisfied with the value that they used to get upon selling their high graded coins.

But the grading system was then upgraded again in 1948, when a professional numismatist, Dr. Sheldon, introduced the Sheldon Scale, which is the 70-point grading scale being used today for detailed identification of the coin's market value. Apart from the MS grading scale, the other parameters in this point scale were:

- **PR (1):** Poor coin
- **FA (2):** Fair appeal
- **AG (3):** About good appeal
- **G (4 to 7):** Good condition

- **VG (8 to 10):** Very good condition
- **F (11 to 19):** Fine condition
- **VF (20 to 39):** Very fine condition
- **XF (40 to 49):** Extremely fine condition
- **AU (50 to 59):** About uncirculated condition
- **MS (60 to 70):** Uncirculated condition or Mint state condition

6.1.4. Grading of the Circulated Coins

The first bucket used in the previous approach was considered the grading range for the circulated coins. In the 70-point grading scale, P-1 to EF-49 is considered the evaluating range. EF-45 is considered the highest grading pointer for a circulated coin. Most of the beginners who intend to get help with their grading, have circulated coins with them. And they are the easiest ones to grade, as no fine observation tools are required for the process.

If you want to try grading the circulated coins yourself, then here are some of the steps that you should follow in order to achieve the accurate results:

- You need a brilliant light source with around 100-watt bulb, fixed to a table lamp. Use a decent magnifier which helps you see the coin with at least 5x magnification.

- Take the three-bucket approach in mind and determine in which bucket seems suitable for your coin. As you are dealing with circulated coins, it will go onto the first bucket.

- Now, you need to use a precise observation to grade the coin based on the narrowed down pointers from the 70-point scale. Describe your coin in the best way possible. Coin that you grade as EF-40 has technically lost only around 5 to 10% of the details, whereas the EF-20 technically lost more than 60% of its details.

It might be difficult for you to properly grade the coins all by yourself. Therefore, it is often recommended to take help of professionals for getting done with the grading part. Following which, you can quote the market value of your coin and sell it over auction, coin events or any other platforms you desire.

6.1.5. Using Professional Coin Grading Services

There are professional organizations offering coin grading services to help coin collectors price their possessions well. In most cases, the beginner collectors out there end up selling their coins without proper grading, which leads them to lose out on profit percentage.

Hiring professionals come at a cost! But the chargeable amount for professional coin grading services varies, depending on the maximum value of that coin. For an instance, if the modern coins are worthy of a value, $300, then the grading cost will be around $15 to $20, which is 5 to 6% of the value.

Now, the percentage also varies depending on the company you choose to grade your coins. Some of the companies offer affordable services, whereas some charge a fortune. You must compare the feedbacks, ratings, and pricing parameters of different grading service providers, before finalizing on one.

Look out for the service providers, who use sonically sealed, tamper-evident and highly secure methods for coin encapsulation. Hence, this will ensure safe storage for your collectible coins, and you can hand them over the job by attaining a peace of mind.

6.1.6. Process for Authenticating the Coins

Authentication is about certifying the specific coins for their genuineness and value. Some most used methods for the coin authentication process are X-Ray fluorescence examination and visual examination. The professional coin graders or certification service providers will be responsible for authenticating your coins.

The independent company will take the coins under their possession and will authenticate its genuineness at first. Following that, the coins will undergo a strict grading process. Once that has done, they will be attributed and encapsulated securely. Thus, once all the reports specific genuine parameters, the coin will be termed as authentic.

The fee for acquiring a certification for the collectible coins, depend on the rarity and expensiveness of them. Under the professional authentication services, you can also pay additionally to get your coin attributed for determining the die varieties. Added verifications, will ensure a higher value is marked for it when you sell it over an auction.

American Numismatic Association (ANA) introduced the coin encapsulation services in 1972 through third-party organizations. It was due to the rising importance of an authentication service for the coin collection industry. This independent third-party opinion is supposed to make a good impact on how the coins are priced in the market. ANACS was found to take over this job. In the next few years, PGCS (Professional Coin Grading Service), also came up to the field for offering similar services, in 1986.

So, you can count on getting your coins certified and authenticated to ensure you don't miss out on the profit potential of your coins.

6.1.7.   Using Price Guides and Other Coin Valuation Resources

If you don't want to spend money on grading, right from the start of your coin collection quest, then you can refer to some pre-written price guides or coin valuation books. These guides have some pre-specified details on certain attributes, which determines how good or bad is the coin that you own.

Depending on the quality assessment parameters specified in those resources, you can determine what would be the average value of the coin when you sell it. There are books and online tutorials available in the coin market to virtually grade your coins yourself.

6.2 Tools Needed for Assessing the Coin Quality or Grade

So, if you are willing to take the grading job onto your own hands, to at least get an idea of what your coin is worth of, then there are certain tools you must have for the job. Remember, when you are grading the coin yourself, you are just determining the value and genuineness of it, in comparison to the quality standards specified within the coin collection market. You are not authorized to authenticate your coin by yourself, as you need an independent and recognized organization to do the needful.

Authentication might not be important for selling off your collectible coins, but it adds a significant value to your particular collection. So, sooner or later, you should consider getting your coins graded by the professionals. But for gaining information right at the start, while buying the coin or understanding its value, you should learn grading it yourself. With the previous section, you are now aware of how to take an approach towards determining the grading of your coins. But, without the right tools, there's a high chance you will be making mistakes in terms of grading the coins.

So, to help you start off with your self-grading quest for the collectible coins, here are some of the tools that every coin collector should have:

- **Gloves**

Are you ready to handle your coins and examine them? The first thing you will need is a pair of gloves. It is quite important for you to touch the coins very carefully, without the need for cleaning them ever. Irrespective of how dirty your coin looks, you should never consider cleaning them, as it would decrease the overall value of the coin.

Apart from that, you don't want to leave contact marks on the coin by touching it with bare hands. Therefore, it's important you use gloves as a prime tool for handling your precious coins. Improper handling might damage the coins and degrade the overall market value.

Human skin releases acids and oils as a natural process, and without gloves you will be rubbing them over the coin, which will degrade the appealing qualities of an ancient or century-old coin. This is something very important when you are handling the uncirculated coins. Soft cotton gloves are probably the best ones for the job, but you can also consider wearing nitrile or powder-free latex gloves.

Apart from the gloves, you should also have a soft pad or cloth for placing the coins and examining them. It is to ensure that if you drop the coin by mistake, the soft pad will prevent it from damage.

- **Gram Scale**

A gram scale is a simple tool that helps you determine the overall weight of the coin. An uncirculated coin will have a proper-maintained weight as determined while it was produced in the mint. But a circulated coin that has been worn out with frequent contact, will have a reduced weight.

The market value, and the condition also depends on the weight difference between a circulated and uncirculated coin of same series. Therefore, it is one of the most important tools that you should own as a coin collector, for determining the grade your coin fits into.

- **Magnet**

Some rare coins are being counterfeited to replicate the rarity and visual elements. With a metal in hand, it becomes easy for you to determine the genuineness of the coin. This should be done before buying the coins, as you don't want to end up paying a fortune for the fake coins.

For instance, the rare copper coins that you own shouldn't get attracted to the magnet, which is the sign of purity for the material. But, if the coin is counterfeited and is polished as copper over the steel coins, then the magnet would attract it, and you must discard the coin, or report a case against the person who sold that to you.

Apart from using a magnet for verifying the genuineness of a coin while grading, you will also need a rare-earth magnet for collecting coins. As a collector, this is one of the most important tools that you should often carry with you to various places where you expect to locate some coins out of luck.

Most of the coin materials used within the past century are made of magnetic materials. So, with a rare-earth magnet, if there is any coin scattered around a site on your excavation trip, this magnet will help collect it for you. You can get a neodymium magnet, which is often found at the teaching resource stores or magic shops. The current United States coins are not at all magnetic, whereas the coins from other countries such as Israel, New Zealand and Canada are.

- **Coin Magnifiers**

When you are grading coins by yourself or are examining a coin before purchase, you will need coin magnifiers as an obvious tool. The standard power of a magnifier should be at least 2X or 3X. But for in-depth grading you might need 5X or 8X magnification. Depending on your purpose, you should get a magnifier that meets the purpose. There are even high magnification tools available in the market, but that won't be much of a use for you, as professionals use them for minute grading requirements.

Most of the professional numismatists use 7x loupe magnifiers for grading the coins, or a jeweler's loupe for identifying the minute die variations. Imagine the level of precision they implement in determining the accurate grade of your coin collection.

- **Other Accessories**

Some of the other accessories or tools that is must for coin collectors to have, includes:

- o **Coin Holders:** In the end, you will always need a tool or accessory to store the coins, so that they can be viewed without experiencing any damage. The beginners have the liberty to use cardboard coin holders that are inexpensive and simple to use. But, if you want more protected storage, then go for some expensive options out in the coin market.

- o **Lights:** You will also be needing great illumination to identify all the details on your coins. You need incandescent lighting for better examination of the coins, than that of the natural or fluorescent lighting. Natural lighting is responsible for hiding small details or imperfections, which deprives you from identifying the core quality of the coin. So, it's better to get a 75-watt bulb or a LED for the purpose.

These are the tools you would need to examine your coins and determine the genuineness of them, all by yourself. You don't have to run to professionals right from the start. You can get the coins authenticated or professionally graded at the time when you are about to sell it off for a profit. But remember that the grading fee is charges based on the current value of the coin in the market. So, if you get the grading and authentication done at the earliest after you own it, you will save a lot of your money. But, if you just want to determine the predicted value of it, before adding it to your coin showcase, then use these tools for self-grading them.

6.3 How to Avoid and Detect the Counterfeits

In the previous chapter, we have already seen the value and rarity of collected coins. Rare coins when collected can be sold for more than its face value and brings in thousands of dollars in profits. To make quick money, a lot of people create and circulate fake coins and sell them at a much higher cost than of its making. This is the process of counterfeit. Counterfeit money or coins are fake coins that defraud people and taint the value of collected coins. An avid coin collector should avoid collecting counterfeit coins. A coin collector should always check for the quality, originality, and history to a coin to avoid counterfeits. In this chapter, you will know more about avoiding counterfeit coins.

6.3.1. How to Detect Counterfeits and Altered Coins?

A coin collector should have the basic skill set of spotting and detecting counterfeit coins not to be defrauded and loses money. Coin collectors spend a lot of money to just buy one coin. Therefore, it is important to ensure that the coin you are buying is original and worth the money you are spending. Counterfeit coins are made without the consent of the official issuing authority.

The coins that are counterfeit are illegal and can land you in legal trouble too. Creating counterfeit coins is an action of deception. The deception of counterfeit coins can cause many losses and fraudulence in the society. Detecting and avoiding counterfeits and altered coins is very important. Before knowing how to detect counterfeit coins, know the types of counterfeit and altered coins.

The types of counterfeit coins are as follows.

- **Cast counterfeits**

Cast counterfeits are the lowest value fakes made. The fakeness of counterfeits is highest in this case. Cast counterfeits are mostly made as a novelty and art not to deceive coin collectors in the process of purchase. Cast counterfeits have a grainy texture and a raised seam where the molds of the cast meet during forging. The cast counterfeits are usually made of base metals.

- **Spark erosion counterfeits**

Spark erosion counterfeits are usually done on coins of smaller denominations. This type of counterfeits is mostly done for copper coins. So, if you are going to buy a rare copper coin check that the coin is not a spark erosion coin. Such counterfeits have a granular texture that you should look for when checking it.

- **Electrotypes**

Electrotypes are counterfeits that are usually created by the museums to display the copy of these coins so that the genuine coin is protected from theft. Both the faces of the coin are displayed by showing the two side through electrotypes. Electrotypes are very close to the genuine coin because they are created by pressing the real coin on a cloth for a negative impression. Electrotypes can be very deceptive and difficult to trace. However, you can detect the coin by dropping it or tapping it. It will not make the same kind of ringing noise a genuine coin makes.

- **Transfer Die Counterfeits**

Transfer Die Counterfeits are coins that are most common in the counterfeit market. These counterfeit coins are difficult to trace too. In the transfer die process, a genuine coin is used to make an exact mirror copy of it. Even the scratches and minute details are copied onto the coin. The depressions and marks make it look like the genuine coin. However, if the coins have the same depressions over and over again, a complete analysis can expose the changes and differences among the coins. Moreover, such counterfeits have a different weight than the real coin should be. Counterfeits also have an unusual level of luster when compared with the real coin.

- **Altered date coins**

The altered date coins are more of altered coins than the counterfeits. Altered dates come up when a particular dated coin is more valuable than a lower value other date coin. Frauds take a much lower value coin and change the date to make it look like more valuable. Altered date coins can be hard to know about because the weight and composition is the same as any other genuine coin of the series, only the date is different. To detect the tool marks related to date change, focus on the date numbers, and look for scratches and smudges.

There are many ways of knowing if the coin is counterfeit or altered. It is true that there are advanced ways of making counterfeit coins, but there are also scientific methods of detecting counterfeit coins. Always check for counterfeit coins before buying it from a person. Ask the seller to share the detailed specifications of the coin. If there are any discrepancies in the specifications and the seller is not clear, then there are chances the coin is counterfeit. Always check for the size, diameter, and thickness of the coin and compare it with the specifications of the real coin. The composition and weight of the coin also matters a lot in determining if it is genuine or counterfeit. There are certain tools that a collector can use to check for the genuineness of the coin.

6.3.2. What is a Foreign Coin?

Every country has been minting coins over centuries and these coins are a part of its history and social evolution.

One country's coins are foreign to the other country. While coin collector does collect ancient and rare coins of their country to keep historical significance, they also like to collect rare foreign coins.

Foreign coins have a value in your native country as these are novel and rarely seen. Collecting coins of other countries that are significant to international and their country's history can be a way of knowing more about the country. Coin collection also includes foreign coin collection. If you are only collecting coins as a hobby, you can start with collecting the low value foreign coins and collect as many foreign coins as possible.

When your collection is complete you can look for rare and old foreign coins that have a lot of history linked with them. Such coins are hard to get but this challenge can only excite an avid coin collector.

There are many types of foreign coins that hold a lot of significance. For example, an ancient coin that dates back to the Roman era and was minted before the fall of Roman empire can be very valuable and rare. Most of these coins are in museums but there could be so many under earth that you might stumble upon. Ancient coins have high face value too because they were almost always made of pure gold or silver. Such ancient gold and silver has very high value today. Ancient coins with the old Roman and Greek gods are the most interesting to look at.

There are other coins like valuable Chinese coins that are also very rare and valuable. However, these coins are not as old as the ancient coins of Roman empire.

Apart from these coins, there are also rare Canadian coins that are very valuable foreign coins. There are many things that are taken into consideration when looking at foreign coins. The people who specialize in foreign coins look for the country's name on the coin. However, in many old and rare coins, the name of the country does not show up.

The language on the coin is also very different from the contemporary language. Foreign coins from different eras are very interesting because they have a different design history, a different minting process and other details in them. Languages like Hindi, Pali, Brahmi, Arabic, and other obsolete scripts can make it difficult to decipher but also increase the rarity of the coin.

While ancient coins are very valuable, keep in mind that even rare modern coins are also valuable. Coins that have been minted by different countries to commemorate an occasion or as a collectible are very valuable.

6.3.3. How to Spot a Fake Coin?

Now that we know about counterfeit coins and that fake coins could be in circulation, we should know how to spot a fake coin. There are many ways of spotting a fake coin.

The top four ways of spotting a fake coin are as follows:

- **Look at the seam**

The dimensions and seam of the coin tell a lot about the coin. Counterfeit coins have casting seam and that can be seen with naked eye. Coins also hold hole markings which can show that the coin is fake. Moreover, when we compare a fake coin with another genuine coin of the series or the image of the real coin, there is bound to be inconsistencies in the coin design. Real coins have some kind of intricate designs that are not found in the fake coins. The Analyzer must look very closely to find these inconsistencies. An irregular seam and inconsistencies are sure signs of fake coinage.

- **Markings and details**

The markings of the coin are unique and rare. The markings that come out of the mint on the coin are its characteristics. The markings that the fake coins have will be different from the markings of the real coins. If you look at the real coins and fake coins, the difference of markings can tell you about the fake coin. There will be some markings of the real coin that will not be on the fake coins. Look at the real coin image and check all the markings and compare it with the coin you have. The markings will not be there or there will be different marks. If the markings match and the seller backs it up with paperwork, then, you can go ahead and buy it.

- **Look at the relief**

The relief of a coin is a very different characteristic that you can look at to know the fakeness of it. The relief of the coin shows the genuineness of the coin. Even when people can counterfeit the coin, they cannot copy the relief. When you look at the relief, the counterfeit coin has either low or too high. When you stack the coin with other coins of the series, if the coin does not coincide with the other coins and the stack topples over then the coin is not real. The coin should be very coinciding with other coins of its series. The coin does not have the same dimension, weight, or features as the other coins of the series.

- **Use a magnet**

You can use a magnet to detect metal coins especially ones made of gold and silver. A real coin that has a high level of silver or gold in it will not be attracted by a magnet. If you know that the coin was supposed to have a high level of gold or silver, then it will not be attracted by a magnet. A fake copy made with cheap metal like iron can be detected with the use of a magnet. If a coin has a silver or gold coating but is made of iron, it can be detected using its strong magnetic property.

Apart from these signs and characteristics there are other ways to detect fake coins too.

6.3.4. Testing the Suspected Counterfeit Coins

There are many techniques to check for counterfeit coins.

The most common ways of checking suspected counterfeit coins are as follows:

- **Use a magnet**

If the counterfeit coin has discrepancies on the front of its real composition, you can check is characteristics with the use of a magnet. Suppose the coin was a gold or silver coin in reality. If you think it is counterfeit, you can take a magnet near it and check for its magnetic properties. If the coin is real and genuine, it will have weak magnetic properties and not attract a magnet. On the other hand, if it is a counterfeit and made of a more common metal like iron or aluminum, it will show magnetic properties around the magnet. Steel and aluminum have silver like appearance and are used to get silver counterfeits. So, one should always be careful of such counterfeits.

- **Check for visual imperfections**

The best way to check for counterfeits is to check for visual imperfections and inconsistencies as compared with the real features of the coin. If you are an avid coin collector with a lot of knowledge about different coins and their images, then, you will be able to notice the imperfections in a counterfeit coin. A lot of counterfeits are really good and almost as real as the real coin. However, they are not as good as the real coin. No matter how real like the coin is, it will have minute differences with the real coin. If the counterfeit is not well made, then the differences are pretty evident. If the counterfeit is well made, you will need a well-trained eye and some tools to detect the minute differences. Close observation of the coin will tell you if it is real or fake.

• Check for their dimensions and weight

Every real coin which has been minted by the official mint of any country, in any historic period will have a consistent weight and dimensions. A counterfeit coin will have some obvious changes in weight and dimensions. Even the minutest change in weight and dimension should be taken into consideration and checked for counterfeit. If the coin is a rare collectible from a much more modern mint that still exists in recorded history, checking its dimensions and weight and matching it with its genuine dimensions will be easy. You should not only rely on the standard kitchen scales for the process. You should get scales that show the weight up to two decimal places. Even if the weight is exact, always check the length and diameter using a caliper and make sure the coin is real.

• Stack the coins

Stacking the coins is a remarkably simple test for counterfeit. If you have coins of the same heritage with you and the new coin is of that series, its relief should also coincide with the relief of the other real coins. Collectors stack up all the coins of the same series to see that they are uniform and stable as a stack. If the stack is uneven and not stable, then the coin that you are putting up is not real. It can also happen if the entire stack is stable but addition of a new coin into the collection topples it over. In this way, you can single out the counterfeit coin from the real ones that you already possess. If you are new to coin collection and the coin is the first of its series to come into your hands, this technique might not be useful.

- **Ping or drop the silver and gold coins**

When you are buying valuable, rare coins, checking for counterfeit is very important. Therefore, the test for silver and gold is very important. For example, dropping the silver or gold coins will create a unique sound. Gold and silver are very different from cheaper metals in their inherent characteristics. Thus, if you are checking for genuineness of a rare gold coin or silver coin tap them and drop them. Also drop an iron or steel coin of modern days to know how a counterfeit will sound. The coin made of gold or silver will have a high pitch long ringing sound that is very different from the dull, low pitch, low frequency sound of the steel or iron metal. When buying a rare coin made of precious metals always perform the pinging or dropping sound to check for the characteristic ring.

- **Place an ice cube on top of the coin**

This is again a test for the rare collectible gold or silver coins. Gold and silver are greater conductors of heat which is also seen in their malleability. Because they are greater conductors of heat when compared to iron and steel, they will start melting the ice cube, the moment it is put on top of them. If the coin is made of cheaper, less conductive materials, then, they will be different in nature. The coin will not conduct heat so soon and the melting process will not start so early as gold or silver coins. This is a very simple test that you can do with only an ice cube. But it is only valid for coins made of precious metals.

6.3.5. Tips on How to Stay Away from Such Counterfeit Coin Scams

As a coin collector, you should be very aware of the differences that set apart real coins from fake coins. Investing in fake coins is a waste of your money and effort as well as your commitment as a coin collector. Therefore, before starting collection of coins, do extensive research into this field and the features and history of coins. The field is a vast field and taking everything in at the national and international level can be difficult. However, with experience and exposure you can learn a lot about how to avoid counterfeit coins. Here are some tips to avoid buying counterfeit coins.

- Always check for the dimensions and weights of the coin. Do not just buy the coin on its features without close observation. Be aware of the dimensions and sizes of different series before you go to buy coins from that series.

- Research about the seller and only buy from trusted sellers. This is especially true when you are buying online. Check for his credentials, his reputation, and the images he has uploaded. Avoid shady deals and trust your instincts. If you can, it is better to avoid online deals, no matter how cheap they come.

- Look for certifications, especially when buying valuable, rare coins of a certain series. Ask and cross question the dealer until you are satisfied and check for the authenticity of the certificates he shows.

With the help of certain tools, tips, tricks, and knowledge, it is easy to stay away from counterfeit coins during a deal.

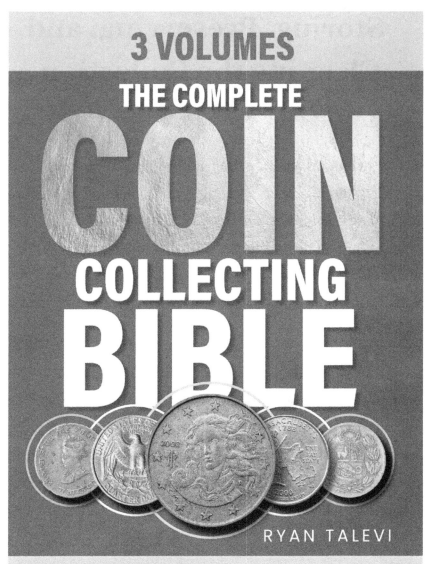

Volume 7
Storing, Preserving, and Cleaning the Collection

It is a strenuous job to gather all of the crucial coins from various sources over several years. But what's more important is to preserve this collection and make it last for generations. Almost everything in this world gets adversely affected as time passes, whether an object or a human. Time deteriorates the appeal and functionality of nearly everything.

And, your coin collection is no different! Not all the coins you bring into your collection have the same shine and mint-like appeal. Some of the coins you collect might be relatively older but must still have the features intact. In that case, you need to take utmost care to store them well to maintain their appeal and quality.

If it deteriorates under your possession, the value you spent on buying it will not be recovered when you plan to sell it out. The coins need desperate protection when they are finally about to rest in your collection after being circulated for a long time.

There's a terrible effect of atmospheric exposure on coins, which fades away the aesthetic appearance of coins. Apart from the atmospheric exposure, some other hazardous elements also corrode the coins over time. As a result, these priceless possessions become waste that no one values.

But there's an optimal way for you to preserve these coins carefully in your collection. You just need to follow the correct procedures to ensure you don't do much worse than good.

You need to be pretty wise to safely store the collectible coins so they travel the future without losing their value. You are now a knowledgeable coin collector with deep insights into how to source, trade, and valuable coins. The only thing that remains from making you a complete coin collector is the right way to preserve your collection.

This book chapter gives you a detailed glimpse into various ways to correctly store or handle your coin. Follow all of the steps, and pass on the knowledge to your fellow coin collectors as well to ensure that the rare coins survive the hands of time and retain their value forever.

7.1 Storing and Preserving Your Coin Collection

To help you retain the value of each coin in your collection, you must follow a roadmap for storing and preserving them. Here are dedicated ways to help you understand what needs to be done:

7.1.1. How to Store Your Coins?

Before we get into how you can store your coins, the first advice for all amateurs is to not wash or clean the coins with any substance. Cleaning the coin will only result in devaluing them. It is because cleaning them with rough substances might cause scratches, add chemical coatings and damage the appeal of the coins.

Not just that, but while you handle the coin during the cleaning process, the grease from your hands will also tarnish the coin when you place it in storage.

The greasing from the hands can be cleaned gently using a lint-free cloth. Apart from that, cleaning is not recommended for collectible coins. But even if you still want to make a coin add shine to your overall collection, then consult a numismatist to help you with the risk-free procedures.

7.1.2. Putting Coins in the Pockets or Envelopes

The use of envelopes or pockets is meant to protect the coins when they are being handled. Following that, it also protects the coins from scratches or dust when they are placed as such in storage. The coins not kept in any envelope or pocket are most likely vulnerable to damage.

So, the next big thing is choosing the right envelope or pocket for the purpose. Irrespective of your choice, the enclosure shouldn't have any acidic properties. Several types of plastics are used today for making storage covers for coins. Some of the common types include PVC, Polyester, and Polypropylene.

Do not go with the PVC material, as it's acidic in nature and will affect the coin adversely over time and degrade it. And as the PVC degrades and leaves its acidic residues, its color will turn yellow and brittle. It indicates that the acidic residues have started affecting the storage environment.

As a result, such mistakes can cause permanent staining on the coins, drastically reducing their value. PVC is the only bad material for storing coins, whereas some other plastics are considered good for the purpose. Among them, Archival Polyester or boPET is a strong material free from acidic properties. This plastic won't degrade like PVC and is ideal for coin storage needs.

The polyester coin pockets are transparent and make the coins visible clearly. The need for handling them without the envelopes is reduced. Moreover, the pockets are also sealed off from the edges to obtain a tear-resistant seam.

In other ways, you can also use paper envelopes for storing your coins. They can store coins but should be free from acid and sulfur contents. The same rule is applied to any glue or adhesive that will be present in the paper envelope.

It is because the sulfur in the paper can potentially damage copper and silver material in coins that turns them black. So, be assured of this assessment while you are using paper envelopes.

Even though the paper envelopes are not transparent, it is easy to write the name of the coin upon them for easy identification. It is a preferable method only if you are not about to show your coin collection to anyone. It is because you will have to remove the paper for a better view, which increases the risk of being dropped and getting damaged.

7.1.3. Storing the Coins in a Dedicated Box

When your coins are already enclosed within a pocket or envelope, you can consider them for storing in a box. The collection will probably be safe from all forms of accidental damage possibilities in a box. Damage to coins is expressed through any harsh impact and due to leakages, floods, pollution, vandalism, or theft.

Therefore, you should consider storing your coin collection in an acid-free box. It is the next step in the quest to protect your coins. Before choosing the box, you should ensure they are in safety pockets or envelopes. While choosing the box, you should consider the material of it on priority. PVC has a reputation for releasing off-gas acids within the storage environment. The coins will degrade upon being in constant exposure to such acids.

Wooden or painted surfaces of the boxes are also acidic in nature, which cannot be preferred for storing your coin collection. You can look out for boxes made up of the same material as the pockets you chose in the previous section. This will ensure the box is free from acidic elements and the coins won't tarnish.

But, if you don't get any such option in the market, you can consider coating the box with plastazote, an acid-free foam for lining the drawers. Apart from that, you can also accessorize the box with a pacific silver cloth, which is a tested material for preventing the silver coins from experiencing any tarnish.

There are reputed manufacturers online who sell quality coin boxes at affordable pricing. They have done all the tests and offer completely risk-free storage boxes without acidic elements. Check out their reviews, study their brand history, and then decide on buying a couple of boxes from them.

When you are using boxes, it becomes essential for you to use indexing cards over them. It is to reduce the overall handling of the coin to prevent accidental damage. If you aren't organizing the collection, you might have to handle it more often for several reasons, which will increase the risks of them getting damaged or exposed to any chemical substances.

Upon storing your coins in boxes, they might just become very heavy. And if you have a hefty collection stored in a big box, it will be very awkward and difficult to move around. Get a medium-sized coin box, which will hold at least 250 coins in them. This is a size that can easily fit into any normal locker or safe.

It is always advised to store the coins in multiple boxes than placing them all in a single box. Use some of the acid-free pads within the boxes to ensure the coins are packed well and won't move within the box. It is because the coins move around while you shift the boxes from one place to another.

7.1.4. Where to Store the Coins?

Now that you have packed your coins well, it's time to decide where you should store them around your property. The area you choose for storing your coins will eventually influence the condition of your coins in the long run. It would be best if you were strict in considering a few important factors while choosing a place to store the boxes full of coins.

Here are some of the tips you should keep in mind for ensuring the longevity of your coins:

- Keep the boxes away from the area where there is a potential possibility of leaks, such as damaged roof spaces, near the windows, or leaky pipes. Any undetected leakage around the property might just cause irreversible damage to the coins.
- It would also be best if you protected the coin boxes from extreme temperatures. The metal coin surfaces might experience condensation if the temperature

suddenly changes from cold to warm. Hence, the roof spaces or unheated rooms aren't suitable.

- It would help if you didn't let humidity settle around the place where the coin boxes are stored. You should avoid all of the areas that possibly have high humidity. Some spaces you mustn't consider for storing your coin boxes are cellars, basements, kitchens, bathrooms, conservatories, and other such spots. Apart from that, avoid storing the boxes against any cold wall.

- Special physical protection should be given to extreme valuables. If you value certain collections more than others, place them all into a separate box, which can be easily stored in a locked safe.

- Ensure the boxes are kept away from any source of air pollution, such as exhaust or paint fumes. The presence of sulfur in airborne pollutants can affect the coins adversely.

With all of these steps followed adequately, you can ensure that your coin collection is now appropriately stored without any possibility of accidental damage or corrosion.

7.1.5. How to Handle Your Coin Correctly?

There will be numerous times when you might have to handle the coins to showcase them to your fellow friends or other coin collectors. When you do, you should follow a specific handling procedure.

When holding a coin, it would be best to go for it by the edges. Use your forefinger and thumb to hold the coin using a soft surface or towel. You can prefer wearing soft cotton hand gloves before holding the coins. It is to ensure that the coin's surface is protected from natural oils released by your fingers. Moreover, the fingerprint marks on the coin can also result in deteriorating its appeal of it by encouraging corrosion.

You might be tempted to polish the coins to make them look shiny, but it needs utmost caution before approaching the procedure. Polishing or cleaning the coins might just reduce the coin's overall value, which we already know. Older coins with natural aging colouration are more demanding in the coin market than those that are polished or stripped away due to improper cleaning.

Apart from that, every time you handle a coin, do it while settling on a chair and keeping your hands on the table. Place a soft towel or a flat cushion that will prevent the coin from bouncing off the surface and crashing down on the floor if it slips off from your fingers.

Improper handling can cause the most damage to collectible coins. Some coins made up of precious materials, such as gold, might be extremely soft. They are very much prone to damage! Even if you hold the coin incorrectly, you will accidentally damage or scratch the coin. Thus, its value will eventually diminish.

The coins have always been pervasive in American Society for several centuries. People from all across the world know the importance of collectible coins. The precious coins need utmost care, which is different from how you treat the circulation coins of today. All of the historic, proof, and uncirculated coins were minted in a minimal amount. Thus, their value for them is very high in the coin market today.

So, imagine you own one, and you just spoiled it by handling it incorrectly and later realize that your mistake made the coin lose its value. You could have got a hefty payout in exchange for the coin you lost because of the accidental damage you did to its appeal. So, if you don't want that for your collection, here are the seven precious rules to sum up the facts of how conveniently you should handle the coin collection:

- Never use bare hands to touch the collectible coins. It is the most important rule of all, which compromises the integrity of your coin collection.

- Never touch the face of the coins, as you will be tampering with the appealing part with dirt, oil, or grime.

- Ensure the coins are in protective holders before you store them in any box after handling them.

- Always ensure a soft surface underneath you while you take the coins in your hands. This way, if the coin drops, it won't hit the floor or experience damage.

- It's better never to clean the coins; in the process, you will expose them to chemicals and touch them improperly.

7.2 Caring and Cleaning Tips for Your Coin Collection

It doesn't matter if you are new to the coin collection or have been in this professional for quite a while now; you will always have the urge to clean the dirty coins. But you also know that cleaning the coins improperly will only deteriorate their market value. So, what can be done? And why is caring for and cleaning your coins important?

Retaining the value of the coins you bought at a specific price is essential. Caring for the coins ensure that the condition of coins doesn't deteriorate any further than the impact of time and handling in the past. Following that, a proper cleaning approach is important to ensure that the features and specialties of a collectible coin don't get washed away due to the use of chemicals or scrubbers.

For ages, most coin collectors don't take out the coins from their enclosed pockets. They believe they care for their coins, but eventually, they overlook their care efforts. If the encapsulated box you used for securing the coins is not of optimal quality, it will seep in small dust particles to stick to the coin's surface and deteriorate its appeal of it over time.

Even the coins that are stored with the utmost care by using perfect storage solutions will develop some form of grime in the long run. If not that, then you might have got a good deal on a dirty coin full of dirt, dust, stains, and grimes. In either case, if you are planning on cleaning the coins, without which it won't add glam to your coin collection, then you should be aware of the possible cleaning options.

Most coin collectors often appreciate any tarnish over the collectible coins. It is because they like the originality reflected in those coins, which were once circulated. Some of the coins are meant to be stored without cleaning: the tarnish over them ensures the authenticity and age of the coins. Therefore, if you are unaware of which coins you shouldn't consider for the cleaning approach, connect with a professional coin dealer.

Consider the professionals' opinion before you accidentally wash away the value of a rare coin. Upon keeping aside the rare collectible coins that demand the tarnish to be intact for retaining a good value, you can head towards the leftover collection of the circulation coins, such as quarters or dimes. You can possibly clean them with a proper approach. Cleaning the coins randomly, without proper guidance, is risky. You might just end up losing your investment!

This book section will discuss the steps and methods you need to adapt to care for and clean the coin collection. Be assured to adapt every step with all considerations intact. Skipping these care measures might lead you to compromise your entire collection, especially if you are a beginner in the coin collection fraternity.

7.2.1. Taking Care of the Collectible Coin

Collecting rare coins has never been an easy task. You must spend time searching for them across various platforms, coin shows, auctions, and dealer showrooms. But, the purpose of a coin collector doesn't end right when they are done finding the specific pieces they intended to. They ought to serve the purpose of holding onto that coin collection by ensuring the value of those coins lasts forever.

And for that, they must take optimal care in handling and maintaining those coins. You might inevitably have to handle the coins multiple times, even after they are in your possession. You might want to shift their location to a different room or examine them to identify the rarity of their features. Irrespective of the situation, you will eventually be handling those coins many times while they are in your possession.

As stated earlier, these coins have already been through a lot of time-oriented circulation wear and tear. Now, when it is in your possession, the value of it depends on how you care for it until you pass it on to someone for profitable pay. All you have to do is take note of a few important things while handling these coins, and you will ultimately be able to show great care to your collection. So, the things you should keep in mind while caring for the collectible coins are:

No Touching with Bare Hands

Right from the time you pay to buy the coin and take it in your hands, you shouldn't use your bare hands. Cotton gloves are the best for use while receiving your coin, and handling them at any time of the day. Most times, if you buy a coin from a reputed dealer or buy it from the coin shows, you will get the coins in secured boxes. The professionals are already aware of what it takes to preserve the coins.

In such cases, you might not have to use your gloves while carrying the coin home, but when you take off the protective case and are about to examine the coin closely, use gloves! Even when you are at the coin shop or show, they will give you a pair of gloves to wear before you touch any of the coins they have put up for sale. If you are a beginner, you might think of these handling methods as a paranoid approach.

But, if you are a professional coin collector or have been through all of the chapters in this book so far, you will understand how the value of a coin is specified by its appeal and texture. Touching them with your bare hands is going to deteriorate it all. The damage you do might not be visible to the naked eye immediately. But, over time, it will showcase the change in texture and color.

Remember, only a few of these coins are left in the market, and the pricing is specified for those collectible coins accordingly. So, if you obtain a coin in a brilliant condition, but do not care for it through careless means, such as by holding them with bare hands, then you will lose its value rather than get an appreciating profit. Hence, wearing gloves is an important part of handling the coins.

From the time you acquire it, store it or handle it again! Make it a habit to never touch the coins without any protective layer around your hands, and don't let anyone else do the same as well. If there are kids around the house who you think might be interested in playing with your coins, keep your collection away from their reach.

Kids can be ruthless towards things they don't understand. At the right age, you need to make them understand the importance of your coin collection and its worth. But till then, it is better to keep them off the area where you have stored the coins.

In Extreme Cases, Use Hand Sanitizer to Clean off the Oils in Your Hands

Despite how strongly we deny you are handling your collectible coins with bare hands, you might be unable to avoid making this blunder. If there comes a situation where you are not with gloves or any protective clothing to safely handle the coin without touching it, make use of hand sanitizer.

If you are a professional coin collector or want to be one, then among all tools you carry, keep a sanitizer with you at all times. Human hands have some oil, which is catastrophic for the rare collectible coins. No matter how rigorously you wash off your hands with water, soap, or other hand-washing solutions, you cannot be sure your hands are free from those oils.

But, as per tests and research, alcohol-based hand sanitizers are quite effective in cleaning the hands and freeing them from oil substances. But this is just for the immediate instance of handling the coins. It means that if you are about to hold a coin with your bare hands at this moment, take out the sanitizer and clean up your hands thoroughly. Only then can you take the coins in your hands and place them back safely.

You cannot expect to wash off your hands with sanitizer once and then get along for hours of handling the coins with bare hands. If you want to handle many collectible coins without gloves, use sanitizer every 10 to 15 minutes. Don't risk letting the oils get trapped on the surface of coins. You might be sure that your hands are clean, but you never know when the corroding oils will return to the surface of your hands.

To help you understand the severity of this, you should know that oil released from the skin builds up over the coin to corrode it. Hence, the metal will develop a tarnish, and the appealing features will fade away. The more you handle the face of the coins with bare hands, the more the chances of subduing their features. Therefore, even though it is recommended not to handle the coins with your bare hands if you do, ensure you are frequently using the hand sanitizer. It will remove those corroding oils from your hands in bulk to ensure care for the coins!

Don't Take Your Hands or Fingers Near the Face

Another way you can avoid destroying the features of the collectible coins by unwantedly holding them with bare hands is by grabbing them by the edges only. If you are not available with any gloves at the moment and are out of sanitizer in your back pocket, there's still a way out. If you want to hold the coin desperately at the moment, make sure you grab the coin by the edges. In any circumstances, do not engage your hands or fingers over the face of the coins.

Such an approach doesn't eliminate the risk of oil spreading over a coin; it will eventually minimize the risk of its buildup over the face. Apart from that, holding from the edges is the right technique to examine the coin and its features. Even if you want to admire the coin, grabbing the coin by its edges will be the best approach.

It is a safe compromise of the coin's condition if you are in a situation where you cannot control the fact of handling the coin without gloves. The edges will tarnish or lose their appeal upon your frequent handling of the coins through this method. But, as the coin market is considered, the dealers, buyers, and other such reputed coin collectors will consider the texture and quality of the face over the edges. So, you will still get good profitable returns for your coin collection.

So, keep these care factors in mind to ensure that you are not wasting the coin, which is one among the last few of its kind.

Add Some Cushioning for the Coin Collection

After giving you a brief understanding of how to handle the coins in different situations through your bare or covered hands, it is time to guide you on the second most common mistake rookie collectors make. Most beginners prefer placing collectible coins on naked table tops. The antique coins are already vulnerable as they have survived the test of time.

Now, if you place them on the naked table without any cushioning, there's a high chance the metal will experience scratches, and the coin will get damaged. Even the slightest scrapes over the collectible coins might deteriorate their grade and value. Therefore, learn from the experts and use cushions or soft materialled trays for showcasing the coins.

You have seen such trays in jewelry shops, which help the base of precious gold pieces to be safe from scratches. You can get similar cushioned trays or cushions for placing the coins over them while you want to examine just to want to place them somewhere. If you cannot source any of them now, use a microfiber cloth or towel to do the needful.

It is an essential step for coins of all types of metals, but it is much more crucial, especially for gold coins. Gold is a very soft metal that may experience damage and scratch due to even the slightest careless handling. The rare silver coins are also vulnerable to mishandling, such as being placed on naked table tops, but are less vulnerable to instant scratches than gold coins.

But, irrespective of the coin material, consider buying a set of cushions to accommodate your coin collection if you are placing it on a flat surface. Most coin collectors prefer to store their coins in glass cases for the guests and visitors to see and admire them. In that case, you should install the cushion materials on the base and sides of the glass case, then carefully place your coins in them. Hence, this is how you should care for the coins that you bought by paying a heavy chunk of your hard-earned savings.

7.2.2. How to Clean and Maintain Coin?

Not taking the mantle of cleaning the collectible coins into your hands is advisable. It would be best to leave it to professionals or not consider cleaning the coins. But if you have a solid urge to store only clean and tidy coins without any residue, dirt, or dust sticking upon them due to the test of time, you should consider cleaning them safely and with the right procedures.

The coins you collect today have been exchanged among various hands over time. An average US quarter stays in circulation for a minimum of thirty years. Hence, it means that more than hundreds and thousands of people might have touched or used it before it settles in your coin collection. So, whether you want to clean off the face to make it appealing or enhance its features and make it more valuable, the cleaning process needs to be precise and accurate.

If you are a new collector wondering if there's any possible way to clean the coins and add value to their appeal, then the answer is yes! But, remember, it is the road less taken, as experienced collectors prefer to maintain the rustic appeal of a coin, to showcase its originality over time.

But, to help you attain the desire of acquiring a shiny collectible coin in your possession, let's get along with the safe cleaning process.

But wait! Before you get along with the cleaning process, you should know a few things about cleaning the coins.

7.2.3. Is there any proficient way of cleaning the old collectible coins?

Some of your valuable coins might have darkened textures, brown films, and green stains. Removing these stains or textures might just degrade its value over time, as even the smallest bits of metal can get chirped off the surface due to its lost strength over years of circulation.

There's no thorough cleaning process available to clean and eliminate the stains completely. The experts agree that cleaning the coins is a big NO!!!

But, retaining the natural appeal without chirping off the coin can add immense value to the overall pricing worth of the coin. But even with all that urge, if the coin is too old, then it is better to keep it away from the cleaning solutions.

7.2.4.   What Coins are Ideal for Cleaning?

The coins that are not too antique and are just a couple of decades older can withstand some form of cleaning intensities. You don't have to go deep with cleaning approaches, such as brushes, scrubbers, and other tools. Going soft with your hands, cleaning gestures, and everything would be best.

7.2.5.   How to Clean the Collectible Coins?

Cleaning the collectible cleans is somehow a tiresome job when you have to be very conscious about how you should keep up with the trend. You can use baking soda for the cleaning process.

You will need two bowls, water, a soft cloth, and baking soda to clean the coins with baking soda. Baking soda ensures the washing process doesn't leave any scratches on the metal. To implement this process, here are the steps that you should follow precisely:

- Firstly, pour the coins into a bowl, and then fill the same with cold water. Make sure the money is well covered while you do the same.

- Now, take another bowl and pour around 1 tsp of baking soda into it.

- Now, you will need a soft cloth to gently wipe off the stains without scrubbing with toothbrushes or hard metal scrubbers. You don't want scratches to ruin the face of the coin.

- Wrap a soft cloth around your fingers, and wipe off the stains as much as possible. You don't have to strain on cleaning it completely. Instead, the mission of your cleaning should be to wipe off the loose dust, dirt, and grimes from the surface.

- Once done, wash the coin in clean water, dry it with a soft cloth, and you are done. Do not re-clean at any cost! The minimal changes you see are all you can get from minimalistic cleaning solutions.

Even though this is a possibility to clean the coins, experts refer you not to try it out at all! You must talk to the experts, show them the coins, and then let them decide if it can go into the cleaning session.

If you are in doubt about whether or not your coin needs cleaning, then you must first get the collection appraised. The collectors usually consider a coin's value based on its appraised value to see if it is significantly higher than the usual intrinsic value. Depending on the appreciation, you can decide if you want to risk cleaning it and deteriorating its value or not.

Unlike the usual everyday coins, collectible coins are no fun or art. You cannot consider ruining the antique possession and damaging one of the only few coins left worldwide. When you own a particular coin with a high-end value, ensure you respect and care for it without negligence.

7.3 How to Maintain the Coins

Maintaining the coins is of utmost importance! When you own a set of collectible coins, you should keep your priorities straight! All you have to do is store the coins safely and keep a tab on maintaining them. There are certain recommendations by professional numismatists on how you can maintain the coins, which include:

7.3.1. Keep it Safe from all Forms of Exposure

It would be best if you kept your coins safe from exposure of all kinds. Whether it is too hot or too cold an environment, keep your coins away from such surroundings. If you have stored your coins in an airtight container, then store them away in that part of your house where there's no water leakage or excessive heat impact.

Even when you access the coins at some point, ensure you are not leaving them naked on the floor overnight without storing them back in their cases. The winter temperatures, rain waters, and summer heat might disrupt the texture of the coin to a minimal extent.

Leaving the coins lying outside without protection will expose them to dust, dirt, grim, and other rough particles, which will settle over them. Later, when you take the coin in hand and mistakenly rub its face, you will end up scratching the material due to rough debris over it.

7.3.2. Get Only the Coin-Specific Storage Pockets

It is advised you should store your coins only in pockets or plastic cases that are made specifically for storing collectible coins. These cases or pockets can protect the coins from scratches or dirt. Using any random plastic box will not be able to prevent air and dust from entering the enclosure, and the coins will keep getting affected due to exposure to various earthly elements.

7.3.3. Clean it With the Use of Baking Soda, Vinegar, Ammonia, Lemon Juice, or Rubbing Alcohol Only

It is restricted to cleaning the coins for most instances, but if you are willing to do the same, use the ingredients mentioned above. They are soft and gentle and don't cause any damage to the old collectible coins upon use. But make sure you aren't using any hard material for scrubbing the surface, as that might deteriorate the face of the coin.

Take suggestions from the experts, and use any mild chemical to remove the unwanted dirt off the face of the coin. It will help you get a clearer and shinier face of your possession. This is suggested only if the above home remedies aren't proficient in order clean the coins.

The value of the coin might just get reduced if you damage the coin during the cleaning process. So, it is gentle advice to all new or old coin collectors to ensure taking suggestions from the numismatists regarding whether or not a specific coin can withstand cleaning.

7.3.4. Coins Made up of Different Metal Should be Kept Separately

The coins that are made from different materials should be stored separately. It is because the coins might clash with one another, and the less malleable metal will experience damage due to the constant hits by the coin made up of high malleability. So, make sure you are using plastic boxes to keep the coins separated from one another. Prefer not to store the open coins in the same box, irrespective of whether they are some metal or not.

7.3.5. Examine the Coins Stored in Envelopes

You must periodically check the coins that you store within the envelopes. It is because the envelopes, even those made of coin-safe materials, will tend to acidify over time. Keeping a constant check on them will help you understand when to replace the envelopes. As a result, you can keep your collectible coins safe for a long time. You can recognize the acidic conversion of an envelope through the yellow spots over the surface.

7.3.6. Use Rubber or Cotton Gloves while Handling the Coins

It is one of the most common and obvious measures for you to maintain your collectible coins. When you need to handle the coins, use only rubber or cotton gloves. In this way, you can ensure that your hands' oils, dust, and stain are not transferred to the coin's surface.

7.4 Potential Causes of Damage for the Collectible Coins

Maintenance of coins is reasonably necessary. Even if you are careful in maintaining your collectible coins, your coins can get damaged in many ways. Being a coin collector, you want to show your precious coin collection to your close ones and other coin collectors. And in the meantime, while showcasing your collection, there is a chance of damage. Here are a few possibilities that you may destroy your coins unknowingly.

7.4.1. Picking up coins with bare fingers

One of the common causes that can damage your coins is touching or picking up your collectible coinage with bare fingers. A human finger comprises acids, minute lines, and oils that can stick to the coinage surface, making the coin lose its color or roughen the surface. The coinages which are known to be rare and of superior quality are more likely to get damaged. You can wear cotton or rubber gloves and carefully pick up the coins to avoid such damage.

7.4.2. Polishing or washing coins

Individuals who are obsessed with cleanliness are likely to keep their coins dirt-free. As a result, they wash and polish their coins to give them a shiny look. However, such a step can lead to damage to your coinages. The coins are made of metal; washing or polishing them might degrade their quality instead of making them good. When you expose these metal coins to the air content, it is likely to get rusted or toned. As a result, the coin will have a harsh texture with an unattractive appearance, lowering the quality of the coinages.

7.4.3. Spitting on coins

When coins are exposed to bare fingers or air, they can get damaged. But spitting on your coins can damage even more. Sounds weird, right? But this is one of the ways the numismatics damage their coinages. When the coins get in contact with the little drops of saliva coming out of your mouth while you are talking, it can make your precious coins have discoloration and leave spots on the surface of coins.

Therefore, you should keep your coins at a distance while talking.

7.4.4. Breaking coin holders

Being a coin collector, you must know or might be having coins stored in holders. Taking the coins out of the holders or mishandling the coin and breaking the holder is a big mistake. The holders act as a protective case for the coins keeping them damage-free. But if the holder breaks, there is certainly a chance of getting your coins' grade value decreased quickly.

7.5 How to Pass on a Coin Collection to the Future Generations?

A coin collector or numismatics is undoubtedly obsessed with their rare collectible coinages. Over time, the coin's value increases, and many coins become rare. As a coin collector, you must consider continuing the coin collection with the next in line. If you store your coins properly, your precious coinage collection shall remain in excellent condition for many generations. But the next in line might not know how to store the coin collections. Therefore, you must guide them properly on storing and preserving the collectible coinages.

Undoubtedly, passing on a coin collection can give financial value to future generations along with the emotions you have carried till now. Having a child who is fascinated by your coin collection and likely to follow your path, it will be easy for you to pass on your rare coinage collections to them. However, if more children have a great interest, disputes are likely. To avoid such disputes, you need to have a clear discussion with them before getting to a conclusion.

Suppose you are unsure about transferring your coin collectibles to multiple hands. In that case, you must decide to give the collection to a single person who can handle and maintain the coinages properly. You can write down the instructions and advice for the coin collection maintenance so they can handle it further.

Children are fond of collections, particularly coins. The rarity of coins makes them more fascinated and attracted to the coin world. They start to research and acquire more information regarding the coins. If your child is keen to learn about your coin collection, you should start sharing your experiences and journey as a numismatic. This makes them determined to their coin-collecting passion and makes them know how valuable collecting coins is.

You can make them practice how to collect coins. Make them teach about keeping records whenever a coin is collected. Make them aware of the scammers, frauds, and thefts they should stay alert about. Ask them to stay updated in the coin market about the values of those coins. Ensure they learn all the necessary information before passing the coin collection responsibility.

7.6 Mint Coins

If you are a beginner in the numismatics field, then you must know the significance of a mint mark on the coins. A mint mark is usually a symbol or an alphabet highlighting where a coin is made. Traditionally, mint markings were affixed to coinages to designate the place that made them in situations with any issues with the metal constituent of the coin. Coining operations were situated in areas with a high demand for coinages and an ample supply of raw materials in the initial years of The United States Mint.

Every year, a specimen of every mint's coinage was delivered to the central mint office. A group of examiners would test them immediately. Each coin piece is measured to ensure it had the correct width and size. The coinage was also measured to ensure they had adequate precious metals. The coinage was then analytically examined to verify the appropriate quality of the metal used.

The examiners could identify which mint site created a particular coin in the event of an issue with it. Next, an inquiry might be started to determine why the in-issue mint plant created coinage that didn't adhere to the correct criteria. Back then, this was crucial when coins were still comprised of precious coins and worth according to how much was contained within. At the moment, the mint markings are more like a concern of history than product testing because modern US coins do not contain any precious metal. In contrast, two versions featured an additional blade on the maize line when a United States Mint facility minted a 2004 half dollar marking the admission of Wisconsin into the country.

Coin production did not involve massive development before the development of sophisticated machines. When done alone, striking needs a person or two, a set of punches, a hammer, and a stock of blanks. A furnace was needed as a component of the bigger procedure for creating dies and heating metals to create the voids. Yet, because these furnaces did not call for highly technical equipment, coin manufacture might be done anywhere, which was advantageous to scammers and areas with a high percentage of recoinages.

7.7 Protecting Your Coin Collection from Loss Due to Theft or Fire

Coin collection is a passion for some people that may be profitable and enjoyable. Coins symbolize a lifetime interest and a physical memory of the development of numismatics for several currency traders, who view them as a lot more than simple assets. But these precious metals are regrettably also a target for robbery; therefore, it is critical to keep your coin collection secured.

The main concern for numismatics is protecting the coinage collections from loss due to theft or fire. Looking for protective cases to protect your collections from burning or theft would be best. Ensuring you get a safe for your collection of coins is the initial stage of safeguarding it. Safes come in various designs, so picking the one that best suits your requirements is crucial.

You can choose a simple fireproof safe if you don't want your coinages exposed to heat. You can keep your precious coins stored in fireproof safes, available in various dimensions and styles to meet your demands. With the fireproof safes, you can rest assured that the coins are safe from burning.

You can choose a biometric safe, which can be a good option if you're searching for a more complex product. The biometric safes have fingerprint scanning that guarantees that only authorized people have the accessibility to the vault.

If you want the highest level of security for your coin collections, you can opt for a gun safe. Many different dimensions and designs of gun safes or vaults are intended to safeguard your coinage collection from robbery and heat damage. Furthermore, they have added security measures like strong locking and solid steel walls built into their structure.

With purchasing the ideal vault for your precious coinage collection, it's critical to ensure that the appropriate security measures are in place to safeguard your valuables. This involves having a surveillance system accessible around the clock every day of the week. In addition, you want to consider putting in alarm systems, surveillance cameras, and other safety features. A suitable security system should be in place at your residence or workplace. In order to achieve this, security glass and deadbolt locking must be installed across all outdoor entrances. Also, ensure that every opening and entrance is secured while not being used.

Ensuring that your precious coinage collection is covered by insurance is the most effective way to keep it safe. You may have an assurance that precious coins are secured in the case of theft, damage, or breakage by getting insurance for the collection of coinage. It's crucial to seek an income protection policy that includes all the assets when purchasing coverage for your great collection. Also, confirming that the coverage fully insures the assessed worth of your coinages is critical. Last but not least, ensuring that the policy covers stealing, loss, and harm is vital.

Volume 8
Documenting of the Coin Collection

Collecting coins is considered a passion, profession, and hobby. And, so far in this book, you have mastered the art of collecting coins from all possible resources. Now, you know how to protect the coins, store them safely, keep them clean, sell them, price them, and pass them on to the next generation.

But, in the quest to secure your coin collection and keep a tab of all of them systematically, you must document them efficiently. Organizing and tracking the coin collection will eventually help you maintain a record of the new coins you bring to your collection and the ones you sell out for liquidating the value. Imagine someone comes up to you and asks to see a coin and price it for buying. But, as you haven't organized your collection, it will take you hours to search through multiple collection boxes to find the one you need.

You might be thinking of this task as a big mountain of stress, but as overwhelming as it might seem, it is easier to make a logical approach towards implementing the same. The specialty of coin collectors passionate about every penny they own is that they like to keep things organized to their satisfaction. They don't want their priceless possessions scattered around like they have no owner. You never do that to the things you own or love!

If you are careless towards your coins, you are probably an accumulator and not a collector!

Maintaining a written record or catalog of all the coins you own in your collection will give you an idea of how far you have come in this journey as a coin collector. With proper cataloging, you will not just be determining the coins you own but will also be able to chart out the future by circling your goals on collecting specific coins.

And if you are willing to pass on your coin collection to the next generation and the generation after that, this catalog will significantly help. Your offspring will get an idea of what you possess and their specific values. So, let's go along with this last chapter of the book and give you a few of the best ways to catalog the coins. This chapter will also educate you on using dedicated coin collection software and its dedicated features.

8.1 Ways of Cataloguing the Coins

There's a specific importance of cataloging the coins, and you cannot deny that. Popular veteran coin collectors believe no one will take these art pieces with them when they die. So, even when you leave this earth, these coins will still be as valuable as they are today. So, to help others, especially those left behind in your family, understand the value of what you have collected so far in your life.

A properly cataloged collection of coins will make it very easy for your heirs to realize how great a collector you are. You might train them in your young days with the importance of coin collection and let them decide whether this interests them. Following that, when you are gone, if your heirs do not want to continue with the passion of coin collection, just like you did, it is their choice.

The catalog you leave behind will help them liquidate the collection by referring to the right market value. The last thing you would expect is to get your collectible coins sold for peanuts that you collected with your hard-earned money and efforts throughout your life.

Besides keeping your heirs educated about the pricing for your various coins in the collection, cataloging is also a legal implication. The IRS demands you show the purchase and sales records for every coin. It is to impose a tax upon them when they are sold. When you or your heir goes out to sell any coin, the authorities will ask you for proof of the original purchasing value or price when it was bought. If you have not cataloged it, then you potentially don't have evidence of the cost of your purchase.

As a result, the taxation authorities will consider any amount you get over the face value of the coin as profit. Thus, the amount will be taxable! It is also considered necessary for you to record any specific coin you have as a reward or present based on the market value at that time. It is important to ensure you don't get strangled in the taxation process while selling the coin.

So, now that you are quite aware of the importance of cataloging the coin collection, let's discuss the ways or methods of how you can approach it:

8.1.1. Documentation of the Coin Collection

All you need to catalog your coin collection through documentation is a three-ring or spiral notebook if you have a small collection of coins. You will need a ruler and a marker pen to make columns for mentioning the details of various coins in them. It is upon you how creative you want to be in documenting the coin collection you own.

You can make as many columns as you want, depending on the type of information you wish to store for each coin. But, some of the basic information that should be present within the documentation folder on priority are:

- Country
- Year
- Variety
- Mint Mark
- Type or Denomination
- Quantity
- Grade
- Purchase Price
- Date of Purchase
- Date Sold (If sold)
- Sale Price (If sold)

It might read like a simple process, but it will take up much of your time with even the smallest coin collection. You need to be very careful while adding information to your documentation folder, as the slightest mistake will be considered a factual parameter of a coin for the next generation who will find this catalog folder.

8.1.2. Use the Acquisition Checklists

Creating an acquisition or coin collection checklist is one of the most prominent ways of cataloging the coin collection alongside deciding upon what coins you would like to acquire next. It will not be based upon any write-ups in a notebook but will be appropriately organized in terms of denomination, mint mark, and type for every series of US coins. You might not get the flexibility of easily documenting the coins, but this method is worth a try.

It is a great initiative when you are just starting with your coin collection. If you have certain goals for collecting specific coins, you can specify them briefly over a documented checklist. Keep striking off those names from the checklist once you complete acquiring them. Leaving the information you already had about the coin, add any specific new details that you get to know about the particular coins you collect. It would help if you did this simultaneously while you collected your coins.

At the same time, if you are collecting any coins you haven't mentioned in the list, you can add them and mention the related information. This way, you won't find it hectic to keep tabs on what coins you own or record.

But, it is recommended that you should use the acquisition checklist method along with the documentation method. It is because, generally, the coin collectors do not add a price column in their checklists. As a result, the coin owners and their heirs will be unable to recall the coin's pricing at the time of purchase. Hence, the IRS will find it difficult to tax the coin when you or your heirs go out to sell coin. Thus, you will be bearing the loss.

So, if you find handling two catalogs of your coin collection troublesome, you can add a pricing column next to the checklist documentation. Follow the process as specified, but keep adding the purchase and selling prices simultaneously to merge the documentation methods into the acquisition checklist. Keep chasing the goal of acquiring all of the coins that you have listed in the checklist over time.

8.1.3.   Use Digital Spreadsheet

The world is now evolving into the digital era, but digital storage of data has been quite popular for a long time. If you know how to use a computer and a Microsoft Excel spreadsheet, then you won't have to keep manual tabs on your coin collection anymore. You can feed your coin collection data, purchase details, and sales details over the digital spreadsheet.

As a result, it will become quite easy for you to add or delete information and create separate sections for different types of coins, existing coins, sold coins, and other such criteria. Adding columns to the spreadsheets is easy with just one click. In this way, if you have any specific information to track or keep a tab off, it will be pretty much easy for you.

Suppose you have different coin folders categorized in terms of types, mints, and other details. Create a specific tab over the spreadsheet for each folder, collection, or album. Now, name each of the tabs the same as the title of your collection folder. Hence, this will help you or your heirs match the folder with the tab in your spreadsheet.

With the digital spreadsheet, it will be easy to calculate how much you have spent throughout your life so far in collecting coins. Following that, you can also calculate the total amount you have earned by selling off a few of your collectible coins. You can implement automated functions to keep totaling the amount every time you add data of a new coin onto the list.

8.2 Online Resources

8.2.1. Using the Coin Collection Software

Now that you are done with the usual and standard processes of cataloging the coins, you will find yourself more organized in your coin collection. But there's another option that you can opt for, for cataloging and organizing your coin collections. And that is by using coin collection software. It is probably one of the best methods you can adapt to document the data associated with your collected coins.

Several software solutions are available for coin collectors to store explicit information about their possessions. You will find many software solutions in the online market to help you with the process. Some of the applications are free, while some are priced at around $20 or $30. If you prefer software solutions from highly reputed companies, then the price might be a bit more expensive for availing of their services.

It will help if you prefer to look for coin cataloging software because of its ease of use, organized screens, and custom organization features. The software will assist you with automatic downloads of the current pricing details and automatic revaluation of the coin collection as per the present market valuation. It would be best if you went with the reputed coin cataloging software provider because you don't want your data to be leaked and misused.

Therefore, it is better not to rely on free software solutions but mostly on paid ones. Even with the paid apps, you should still consider their reviews, check their security policies, and review other such parameters before you can finally decide on counting on them. Using digital software will help you stay updated with the technological trends and also ease your logistical load of managing and cataloging the coins.

But, there are a few things associated with using the coin collection or cataloging software that you should use on priority. Such features would help you better track your coin collection over the software and get better insights into other such information.

8.2.2. How to Use the Online Resources and Database?

The coin collection software often has direct access to various coin databases and resources. Find the dedicated options on the main page of the applications, and you will be redirected to genuine resources upon various collectible coins. You can use these resources to gather sufficient information on specific types of coins and determine whether you should add them to your collection or not.

When you are ready with the available information about the coin you are looking for, try locating the same in the linked database that connects with a valid website or server with updated data on the various details of select coins. In some of the dedicated coin cataloging applications, you will get a linked database of coins that will indicate their availability.

It means you can check out the data on where the coins are available, with which dealer, or with which collector. Based on the data, you can consider approaching acquiring them. If not the availability, then you will mostly get insight into the appreciated pricing of the coin compared to its value in the past years. Hence, you can determine if the price appreciation is good enough for you to consider as an investment.

Hence, the online resources and database within the application will greatly help you bring new coins to your collection with ease.

8.2.3. How to Use Coin Certifications and Grading Services?

Numismatic Guaranty Company (NGC) is an authority that receives around millions of coins from collectors and dealers for certification and grading. Many other reputed authorities are responsible for authenticating, grading, and certifying the coins, but NGC is among the top names. The strength of NGC guarantee will help you earn a good value from your coin.

Whether you are hiring NGC or other top-tiered grading or certification agencies, you must first send them the coins via shipping. You need to pack the coins properly and make sure that the coins don't experience damage during transit. If you live close to the grading or certification centers, you can personally hand over the parcel to the authorities.

Once the graders receive the coins, they will carefully verify the coins and their quantity and report the same in their records. When the coins are done being counted, they will then be inspected, and they will be updated in the database. And then, the coins will be sent for grading.

The coins will now be examined and undergo certification by several professional graders. Professional firms engage more than one grader upon a single batch of coins. The date, mintmark, denomination, variety, designation, grade, and UIN will be identified and labeled. Once the coins are graded, they will be stored in protected holders with a unique label.

Once the grading is done, the coins will be sealed sonically within the two plastic shells to ensure utmost protection. Hence, this process is called encapsulation. Once the coins are graded, certified, and encapsulated, they will be sent for the final round of inspection, before the shipment is prepared to send back to the owner.

Hence, this is how the grading services are approached! The best thing about being a coin collector in this digital era is that you don't have to spend much time finding the right grading service provider. If you are using coin cataloging software from a reputed provider, then there will be an option where you can access top grading service providers.

You are just one click away from checking out the process of getting your collectible coins certified.

Once you have raised your grading request, you will be sent further information on how you can ship your coin collection to the certifying or grading authority.

8.2.4. How to Use Coin Collecting Forums and Communities?

As you have taken your coin collection passion to digital software, staying connected with the community won't be much of a hassle. The dedicated coin collection software has community accessibility, like social media for the coin collectors. In such applications, you can interact with like-minded coin collectors. You can discuss trending coin collection tips and might be able to source some of the rare coins with some collectors.

The same applications also have forum sections for people to post their thoughts, answers to questions, and queries on different coin collection topics. Even if you don't find one linked to the application, you can still find a lot of active forums across the internet. Being part of active coin collection communities will help you stay updated with the fluctuating value of specific types of coins. Apart from that, you will also learn a lot about rare coins, fueling your passion for coin collection.

8.2.5. Showing Your Coin Collection

Finally, when you are done collecting and cataloging your coins, you should participate in some other events associated with a coin collection, such as selling events. You can take your coins to dedicated shows or events, both physical and online, where you will display the coins for audiences to see, admire and buy.

If you are new to the coin collection market, you should keep a few things in mind to show your coins properly to veteran and new collectors. Properly displaying your coin collection is a challenge. You must ensure that your coin collection is safely and securely displayed. As you present the coins to a big audience, you must make the display aesthetically pleasing and admirers.

8.2.6. Points to Remember While Attending Coin Shows

So, if you have decided to attend your first coin show, you should be aware of a few things. So far in life, you have collected coins of all types, dates, and values. This will be the first time you will set up your counter to display the coins and will be open for selling off your select coins. Here are a few points you should consider on priority to survive your first coin shows proficiently.

1. Maintaining the Coin Show Etiquette

Etiquettes are of utmost importance when you are attending the coin shows. Here are some of the etiquette advice for you to rock your first coin show:

- **Wear Proper Shoes:**

It would be best if you got proper boots to create a great impression among the famous coin collectors who will be there to see your collection and buy. Shoes reflect the overall personality you carry. So, participating in the coin shows with an old, unpolished pair of shoes will get you a bad name. People might not trust your professionalism, seeing your attire and how you present yourself. So, don't let the valuable personalities lose sight of you when you are displaying your coins in a coin collection show.

- **Bring Cash with You:**

It isn't a good gesture when you sell off coins and don't have change money to return to the buyers. Therefore, make sure you have cash along with you to sell off the coins without the cash crunch. Keep multiple payment options available to you to address the flexibility of the buyers.

- **Use Your Catalogue:**

Use the catalog to share information about the specific coins the buyers or admirers would request. You don't want to fumble at the time when someone asks you the blue question about the coin. If you have cataloged your coins, it will be easy for you to retrieve the information immediately.

- **Don't Flaunt the Purchases:**

You don't need to flaunt the purchases you have made in the past. It would be best if you were gentle while displaying your coins to the people who visit your counter. If you try flaunting your collections, people will mostly create a wrong impression of you. Following that, you will not be well-praised within the coin collector fraternity.

- **Always Bring Your Own Tools:**

You ought to bring your own tools to the coin show, as asking others might make you look unprofessional. Coin loupes, magnifying glasses, light setup, and other such tools are essential for you and your visitors to the counter for inspecting the coin. Keep a set of rubber gloves to offer to the visitors for inspecting the coins.

2. Joining Online Coin Collecting Communities

There are various online coin collecting communities where that host online coin shows. If you are part of such communities and want to showcase your collection to like-minded coin collectors worldwide, then await the right opportunity. You need to click good pictures of your coin collections and make a presentation slide of all of them.

In most cases, the presentation slides display the coin collection, where the collector will explain each collection through a video meeting session. Some online coin collecting communities host an event where every member is asked to display the best coin in their collection. In a video conferencing call, the owner will display the coin live.

In this way, joining online coin collecting communities will help you showcase your coin to a larger audience. It is even better than selling off the coins over a coin show. You don't have to worry about any etiquette or rules & regulations around the community. Certain community policies might be for all the members, but they aren't as strict as that physical coin shows.

You need to maintain the proper care and handling routines to show your coins. While presenting a live coin on a conferencing call, ensure you have to cushion underneath the base where you are sitting. Don't let accidents ruin the value of your priceless possession. Apart from that, use gloves and hold the edges. In this way, you will be able to show how professional you are in the arena of coin collection.

3. Using Online Coin Marketplaces

You can use online coin marketplaces to try and sell off your coin collections. You don't have to be part of the physical or online coin shows to display and sell your coins. You can list them over several online marketplaces where people actively seek collectible coins.

You must ensure that your list's pricing is the best per the market value. The people who know the actual value of the coins in your collection will definitely be buying coins from you.

Like all other online marketplaces and e-commerce websites, coin marketplaces are also in demand. It wasn't easy to trade coins and increase your coin collection earlier. You had to meet people physically and buy coins after much negotiation. Selling coins was also an extensive process earlier.

However, websites and digital marketplaces have simplified the coin selling and buying process. There are many trustworthy coin marketplaces that you can visit and look at the coins offered. Such websites and e-commerce marketplaces make the coin collection process very easy.

When selling coins, make sure you are connecting with a genuine buyer. Similarly, when buying, make sure you connect with a genuine seller offering authentic and valuable coins. The effort put in by the coin collector to find the coins he wants is reduced by the online marketplace.

Moreover, today, such marketplaces have more flexibility and security of payments. You can conduct the transaction securely and safely and get your desired coin at home. The process on online platforms reduces the effort, time, and money spent on getting collectible coins. Such websites also offer the option of auctioning on the platform to buy and sell coins on your own terms. When looking at such websites and marketplaces, check their reputations and talk to your contemporaries. Go for recommended coin selling and buying websites that many coin collectors use.

There is always a risk of getting scammed at online marketplaces because of reduced visibility. However, you can choose to buy or sell on reputed websites and deal with only verified profiles after communicating with them.

8.3 Understanding the Coin Dealer's Point of View

Coin dealers are also important in the coin collection hobby circle. Coin dealers are people who find old and rare coins for coin collectors and sell them for money. They also buy coins from coin collectors when they wish to sell them. A coin dealer has his own network and sources coins for deals selling and buying. The coin dealers may or may not be coin collectors, but they act as agents for coin collectors in finding a rare coin and buying or selling it to interested parties. The coin dealer keeps coin collectors in his contact list and sells particular coins to people willing to pay the price he is asking for.

Coin dealers put a price on a coin and convince coin collectors that it is the actual price of the coin. Their profit is the margin between the actual price and the price they quote for their clients. Coin collectors pursue the hobby as a passion and are less worried about the coin's value. Coin dealers have more knowledge of the market and help estimate the worth of any coin. Often coin collectors either overestimate or underestimate the value of their coins. In such cases, they consult with a coin dealer and get to know the real price of the coin. Consulting with a trustworthy and honest coin dealer is important to get the right information and get a good deal on coin purchases or sales. Coin dealers are like agents between the coin buyer and seller and coordinate the sale.

As a coin collector, you might look at the process as a hobby, but for a coin dealer, buying a coin is a risky decision. He places his risks on a coin when he spends a lot of money buying a coin. He then has to increase the price of the coin for the prospective buyer so that he gets his money back and makes some profits. He can then invest this profit in buying more valuable and rare coins and selling them to interested coin collectors. Like coin collectors, coin dealers have to beware of scams. When buying a coin from a collector or a seller, the dealer has to look at the quality and rarity of the coin and then buy the coin for a good price. Sometimes, the collector might demand more money when compared with the actual price of the coin. The coin dealer has to deal with such a situation cleverly to avoid scams. While avoiding scams, the collector must stay on course to buy the coin because the collector can go to any other dealer to sell his coin. The coin dealer has to maintain a balance between customer service and profits.

The coin dealer has to be knowledgeable and experienced. He sometimes has to be more knowledgeable than the coin collector. He must keep updating his knowledge about coins and the rules of purchase and sale of coins to stay within the legal limits. From the coin's visual to its details and dimensions, the coin dealer has to remember and record everything to bargain and deal with coin collectors. If the coin dealer is not well-versed in the market and does not have the trust of coin collectors and enthusiasts, he loses his customers and fails to make a mark in the profession.

The coin dealer should possess coin and currency knowledge and market knowledge. To make profits and help coin collectors make market-related decisions, he should know about coin market trends and predict the market's future. When he can grasp the short-term and long-term future of the market, he can sustain himself in the profession. The coin dealer needs to be patient and have strong financial knowledge. The network of the coin dealer and the type of coin collectors he knows are major contributors to the profit-making ability of the coin dealer. If you are going into the profession of coin dealing, focus on creating a complete network of coin collectors and enthusiasts and building your knowledge base in the field from the ground up.

Volume 9
FAQs

9.1 Do's and Don'ts of Coin Collecting

Learning the art of coin collecting requires patience. The most crucial thing to remember is that you are engaging in this activity for the correct reasons; if you desire it, you should go for it.

Although collecting purely for financial gain may be effective, it rarely serves over the long term. Many individuals who have attempted it for that purpose have lost momentum and failed, so one must seriously consider the options. Regardless of how or what you decide to begin collecting, there are a couple of dos and don'ts that really are important to remember to prevent dissatisfaction and excessive investment.

Professional coin collectors invest considerable time in becoming experts in numismatic coins. Excellent informational resources include publications, newspapers, and brokers who may share information as it arises. Using the resources, one can move quickly to prevent information from being obtained first by rival collectors with the same goal.

9.1.1. Do's:

The following are some tips you should perform while collecting coins:

Perform an in-depth search before purchasing

The coinage marketplace is likely to fluctuate, just like other trading categories. Not all coins make wise investments. If you are a beginner and enter the coinage field without researching the coinage market, there is a higher possibility of getting scammed. But for individuals with the correct mindset and knowledge, gathering rare coins may be rewarding.

Choose a seller whose credentials are correctly verified

When you don't purchase costly products from your local street vendors in fear of being scammed, then why would you purchase such rare and precious coins from sellers who are unknown to you? Therefore, if you want to be certain and confident that the coin you are purchasing is real and original, you must consult a trustworthy, knowledgeable person. You can approach your insurance provider for recommendations or see a group of sellers who are members of the Professional Numismatists Guild at PNGdealers.com.

Verify the coin's integrity

Even though a coin could appear to be the real deal when seen in person or through the internet if you're unsure of its genuineness, get it graded by an outside expert. Since a grader will have no financial incentive to buy or sell coinage, they are neither buyers nor sellers. You may locate a qualified grader using the Professional Coin Grading Service (PCGS). These coins are stored airtight in a plastic container with inside labeling and have a PCGS certification.

Store coins with safety at home

Smoke from tobacco, latex, paint, fabrics like wool, and excessive moisture may cause coinage to degrade. Use airtight plastic carriers, including the encapsulation blocks provided by independent grading companies, to preserve the coins excellently. After that, store those for safety in a safe location, such as a bank deposit box. Unsecured coins become easy targets for intruders entering your house and stealing your precious coins.

Get insurance plans

If you are a coin collector, you must know their valuation. Therefore, you must protect your precious coins with insurance coverage, just like the rest of your assets. Avoiding such plans could lead to a great loss. Getting insurance coverage for your coinage collection can ensure that they can be replaced or restored if they are lost, robbed, or damaged. You can search for a useful policy that offers no-deductible, international, and all-risk insurance coverage. Some insurance might also offer a certain amount of immediate coverage for recently purchased coinage.

9.1.2. Don'ts:

The following are the few things you should avoid while coin collecting:

Dont try to clean your coins

If you are simultaneously a coin collector and a hygiene freak and want everything clean and tidy, you should avoid washing your coins. Washing and polishing the coins can lead to harm. It can also take away the coin's natural shine or mint shine and significantly lower its value. Coins that have undergone polishing, washing, whizzing, or somehow changed generally attract values equivalent to two grades less than they might have. For instance, a polished, exceptionally fine (XF) quality coinage will probably sell for more money than one rated as Fine (F). it is best to keep your precious coins in protective cases specifically created to safeguard them.

Avoid selling to pawnshops

Several shops typically place ads saying that they purchase gold and any metal. Most of the time, these businesses and ordinary gold purchasers are not competent to recognize the rarity of your coin collections, which have more value beyond their metal composition. Such businesses are unaware of the Sheldon 70 grading method, where coins could be appropriate for third-party rating, the difference between mintmark and perfect coins, rarity, and the valuation of the coins. If you sell your coins to these types of shops, you might end up paying hundreds of dollars. If you just deal with unique bullion in the shape of frames and circles, it might not matter as much, but concerning the coins, it's crucial to work with a skilled coin specialist.

Don't sell your coins too quickly

Before selling your precious and rare coinage collections, ensure their valuation in the coin marketplace. You might face a more significant loss if you sell your coins before researching their current value. You can approach a coin specialist, who can guide you regarding the market prices of your coins so that it's easier for you to decide to sell your coinages at the right time.

9.2 What do you mean by Numismatic Language

The word "numismatic language" describes the specific terms and language associated with researching and collecting coinage, medallions, and other types of money. In addition to phrases designed to automatically convey the contemporary setting and historical importance of various coins, this terminology also comprises particular terms for explaining the actual properties of coinage, such as their dimensions, mass, and metal constitution. There are many words and ideas used in numismatics that are associated with the creation, development, and historical importance of coinage. It enables communication regarding coins and their properties between experts, passionate, and collectors in a straightforward way.

Coins and other forms of money are written in the native language. The languages used on coins reveal much about the world's history: French, notably English, is used everywhere, while the Western Hemisphere contributes significantly greater Spanish and Portuguese than Europe. How various countries are presented, which may not be identical in all languages, shows another aspect of linguistic diversity. It can sometimes be simple to translate; "Brasil" definitely refers to Brazil, while "République Française" refers to people who speak English as France.

Numismatics may be enjoyed by anybody, regardless of their language skills. Yet, after learning about the numerous, diverse ways that coins and money are described in English, you could even begin to resemble one. Most European languages, including English, utilize the famous Latin alphabet, although other nationalities use unique characters. For instance, Greek and Russian letters contain well-known and uncommon characters. Hebrew, Arabic, Japanese, and Korean, as well as the character-based depiction of Chinese, are languages that are further away. Even in places where English is not officially recognized or commonly spoken, there are significant linkages to English in the globalized trade of the twentieth and twenty-first centuries: practically every country uses the same Number system seen in American currency.

Language itself occasionally turns into a topic for numismatic study. Interaction is tough in the European

Union, where there are a lot of different nations, cultures, and writing systems. Keeping the system as straightforward as reasonable considering the situation is the obvious response to this complication. Euro and Cent are the sole letters upon these same sides of the coinage. However, multilingualism falls short compared to India, where currency notes are written in 17 distinct languages. There are 15 other national languages on the rear, along with Hindi and English on the front.

9.2.1. What are the terms referring to the condition of a coin?

Generally, coin collectors can believe that a coin must appear provided how well the coin's quality is defined if:

- coin grading is performed using descriptors

- and a 1-70 numerical grade

- rules have been created appropriately to make this true.

Different terms refer to the condition of a coin described:

Poor (PO-1): Hard to identify. The design will have a significant percentage of flat surfaces. The date can be hardly noticeable or not present at all. It is also termed as Basal State.

Fair (FR-2): Rims have been well-integrated into the design. A few graphic lines must be present along the coin's surfaces. However, the writing can be totally missing. The coinage must be identifiable if a sufficient portion of the date is clear.

About Good (AG-3): Most of the coinage's pattern will be highlighted. However, the text or symbols will typically be somewhat hidden by the rims' wear and occasionally known as Almost Good.

Good (G-4, 6): It will include a basic overview of the coin's appearance. However, there won't be much precision, and some might be deeply flawed. The rim often will still be present, although, in rare instances, it might have worn down towards the heads of the characters or symbols. Non-collectors frequently describe their coinage in the "Good" state category, despite the fact that Good coins are significantly worn.

Very Good (VG-8, 10): Although the coinage will show moderate to high wear, sure of its patterns remain visible. For example, three or more letters from the word LIBERTY can be found on seated coinage, Liberty Nickels, Barber coins, and Indian Head Cents.

Fine (F-12, 15): The coinage will show moderate wear with several features still noticeable, as well as some high places that are clearly decayed. For example, the seven alphabetical letters of LIBERTY will typically be observed on sitting coins, Liberty Nickels, Barber coins, and Indian Head Cents: However, some might be quite faint.

Very Fine (VF-20, 25, 30, 35): All general features on the coinage may become prominent, displaying moderate to low total deterioration. For example, the seven characters of the word LIBERTY may become completely visible and powerful on sitting coins, Barber coins, Liberty Nickels, and Indian Head Cents.

Extremely Fine (XF-40, 45): Less erosion can be seen on the top places of the coinage. There can also be a hint of mint shine. It is often shortened to EF.

About Uncirculated (AU-50, 53, 55, 58): The coinage shows moderate to almost complete shine with erosion that ranges from hardly noticeable to barely a hint of roughness on the highest places of the coin surface.

9.2.2. What are the terms referring to coin features?

Two terms refer to coin features, namely, observe and reverse.

Observe: Observe is a term in the coin terminology used to describe the front face of the coin. Since it frequently features the head of a famous public figure, the observation of a coinage is referred to as "head". Typically, the face of a coin with the bigger picture is referred to as the obverse.

Reverse: Reverse is a term in the coin terminology used to describe the back or rear face of the coin. Reverse is the opposite side of the observation, featuring a smaller picture. Most coins have details about their usage as a means of trade on their reverse side, including the coin's value. The reverse is also referred to as "tail".

9.2.3. What are terms referring to mint places?

A mint is a significant supplier of a nation's coinage and is authorized by the government to create coinage that can serve as a medium of exchange. The mint manages its different manufacturing facilities, produces and distributes money, safeguards its resources, and manages its operations. The United States Mint is a self-funded organization that was established in 1792. The San Francisco Mint issued 50-centavo silver coins for Mexico in 1906, demonstrating that a nation's mint is not necessarily situated within or even controlled by the nation.

Mint state: An uncirculated coinage that is in perfect shape and shows no traces of use. However, it could have minor traces of storage in bags before being sent by the mint to the government facility.

Mintage: A mint's entire production of the coinage of a specific denomination, period, and kind is known as its mintage. The mint informs customers how many silver coinages are being produced. Coins in the Mint State are simply matte-finished and frequently contain little flaws from arranging during the minting procedure.

Mint marks: A coinage's mint location may be determined by its mint mark, a letter. They consider a coin's manufacturer to be accountable for its integrity. When the United States made circulating coins from valuable materials such as gold and silver, a committee examined the metal combinations and the quality standards in the coins produced at each Mint location.

9.2.4. What are the terms referring to denomination?

The term denomination is frequently utilized to refer to a measure of a price or numeraire assigned to currencies such as notes and coinages in addition to other financial tools with fixed values involving notes issued by the government authorities. Because it is printed on the face or the front side of the currency, the denomination is also called 'face value.' Based on the location, the period, and the objective of the coinage, denominations might differ, which is determined by its face value, such as:

Cent: A coin with a face value of one-hundredth of a dollar and is utilized throughout the US and other nations.

Penny: A coin that is legal currency in the U. S. and a few other nations and has a face amount of five cents.

Nickel: A coin that is legal currency in the UK and a few other nations with an original amount of one-hundredth of a pound.

Dime: A coin with a face worth ten cents is utilized in certain nations, including the US.

Quarter: A coin that is legal currency in the United States and a few other nations and has a face amount of 25 cents.

5. What are the other terms under numismatic?

Here are some other specific terms for numismatics.

Exonumia: The term Exonumia refers to numismatic objects involving tokens, scrips, or medals, except for notes and coins.

Notaphily: The term Notaphily refers to the study and gathering of paper money. The word is the fusion of the Latin term 'nota', which means paper money.

Philately: the term Philately refers to the study of the history of postage stamps. It also describes the purchase and satisfaction of stamps and other philatelic items.

Scripophily: The term Scripophily refers to gathering old stock documents, bond certificates, and other financial papers for historical significance.

9.3 Recommendations

9.3.1. What are the recommended coin collecting books and **publications?**

There are many books and resource materials that you can read and delve into if you are going to start coin collecting as a hobby.

Some of the best books that you can read are as follows.

The Red Book- R.S. Yeoman and Kenneth Bressett

The Red Book is an excellent official book if you have started collecting coins and are interested in American coins. The Red Book has been under annual publication since 1947. A magazine like Red Book includes the coins' pricing and the historical background of each coin collection. The book also contains the photograph and mintage data of every coin made from the US American coin series. Coin collectors can use this handbook to compare real coin images and complete a collection.

Whitman's Guide to Coin Collecting

The Whitman Guide to Coin Collecting is a guide for beginners in Coin collection. The guidebook includes mint marks, varieties, value, and collection maintenance tips. If you are a beginner in coin collection, you must grab this book.

The Coin Collector's Survival Manual

The coin collector's survival manual from Scott A Travers is a good book on coin collection. It is recommended because it is written by one of the most knowledgeable coin dealers and former consultants of the Federal Trade Commission. You can learn about the new coin grading system and avoid scams while buying coins from dealers.

the 2020 Standard Catalog of World Coins

The 2020 Standard Catalog of World Coins is a complete guide to 20th-century coins and their details. If you want to learn about the modern coins in human history before collecting them, you should buy this massive catalog of coins.

One-Minute Coin Expert

The one-minute coin expert is a book that will give you the essential details about coins and coin collection. This book lets you recognize valuable coins in your pocket change.

9.3.2. What are the recommended coin collecting websites and online resources?

There are many official and commercial sites and online resources that you can visit if you are investing in coin collection. The top websites you should visit are the United States Mint, PCGS CoinFacts, Newman Numismatic Portal, and CoinNews.net...These websites offer information about genuine coin series and help you buy authentic and rare coins. CoinNews.net and other official websites also provide news and blogs about coin collection and release.

9.3.3. What are the recommended coin collecting software and apps?

The coin collection process has become very advanced and technical with the help of software and apps. There are many apps and software that can aid you in the collection of coins. These are specially designed to detect coin changes and fraudulent copies of authentic coins. Coin collectors have become smart and use software and apps for coin detection and collection. One of the apps is the PCGS set registry which helps keep records of your collection across multiple devices. The app is used to complete achievements and get points as you complete a coin collection. Another app that you can keep as a coin collector is Exact Change. Exact Change has extensive databases of coins and collectibles across different countries that you can refer to when collecting coins. Another Ezcoin is a coin collecting software that can track your coins and tell you the values of the coins. Ezcoin can be used to organize your coin collection and track the value of the coins.

9.3.4. What are the recommended coin collecting communities and forums?

When you start a coin collection, you will join the coin-collecting community of the world. The coin collection community exists in real life, and you can contact your fellow coin collectors via the internet and social media. Many coin-collecting communities and forums today support discussions and communication related to coin collection. Such forums connect you to a larger community and help you gain experience and insight into the coin collecting hobby. After starting your journey as a coin collector, join at least one platform for coin collection and discussion with your contemporaries. This will expand your view of the hobby and the community. Some well-known coin collection communities are Coin Talk, Collectors Universe, Numis Forums, and CAC forums. Such online forums allow you to interact with other coin collectors and share information and pictures. As a beginner, you can gather a lot of knowledge from active participation in such forums.

9.3.5. What are the recommended coin collecting museums and institutions?

Museums and institutions also play a huge role in preserving and circulating rare and authentic coin collections. Such institutions trace the history of rare coin collections and keep them intact for enthusiasts to see. Museums and institutions protect our history and allow us to secure a window into the past. Many coin collections and rare coins have been created alongside historical events of the world. Museums and institutions with rare coin collections keep such stories and events alive in our memories. Many museums and coin collections have extensive collections of rare and historic coins. Even if you are not an active coin collector, you should go to the nearest coin museum and explore the beauty and history of world currency. If you have time and the money to explore, visit famous museums like the National Numismatic Collection of the Smithsonian Museum. The National Numismatic Collection is the world's largest collection of coins and money used in transactions. The museum holds a lot of coins from the American Mint and the US money collection. Another famous museum is the American

Numismatic Association (ANA) Money Museum, known for its Harry W Bass collection. The Eliasberg Collection is an old private collection from the 1920s to 1950s. The Elisaberg collection is enormous, and at one point in time, it had a valuation of US$60 million

Conclusion

Coin collection or Numismatics is an age-old hobby and habit of people that have existed for many centuries. Avid coin collectors have left their legacy in the form of large coin collections that are still displayed as exhibits in museums and institutions.

If you are searching for a long-term hobby that challenges and inspires you to improve, you should start a coin collection.

People who recognize the worth of money and are very interested in human history know that the history of money is intertwined with anthropological history. Money has remained timeless as humans have transacted and bartered with each other since time immemorial. Therefore, coin collection is a timeless hobby that can bring you a lot of fulfillment and happiness.

If you start small and stay dedicated to the coin collection hobby, you can even get fame and recognition as a coin collector. The coin collection hobby has been called the Hobby of Kings. Coin collection is so much more than just a hobby. It is a way of preserving our history and looking back on the most important parts of our history.

Collecting coins and gathering information about them is our way of reflecting on the lifestyle of our ancestors and knowing more about their way of living. Throughout history, coins and rare collectibles have marked the changes that have come upon countries and humans. By collecting these rare coins and transactional materials, people can get a window into the history of humankind and the evolution of society. Coin collection is a hobby that will never bore you because there will always be new coins to collect. It can also be exhilarating because you never know when you will stumble upon a rare coin. It could be possible that you find a rare or old coin on the road. Many people think that old and ancient coins hold no value. To the eyes of the coin collector, every coin piece and any old coin can save a lot of value.

To know the coin's value, you have to delve deep into the history and making of the coin. Moreover, you do not have to invest a lot to start collecting coins. You can start collecting coins by asking your friends and family. You can search for currencies of different countries and collect coins from each country if you have friends living there. Once you start collecting coins, your passion will only increase. Today, it is elementary to start out as a coin collector. You can use coin-collecting software and databases to learn about the rare coin collections you can make. You can also use the apps to organize your coin collection and track its value.

Coin collection is a fascinating hobby because it opens up a new world for us. It connects us to a larger community and makes us a part of intellectual conversations around history and culture. The habit of coin collection can reward us with knowledge and valuable assets if done correctly.

Join the coin collection community today and start making your collection from scratch.

References

https://www.thesprucecrafts.com/mint-error-coin-768452

https://historicalmedallions.com/blogs/news/ten-types-of-medals-and-medallions-that-should-be-on-your-collectors-list

https://www.coinnews.net/tools/error-coin-price-guide-with-mint-error-photo-descriptions/

https://www.royalmint.com/discover/coin-collecting/beginners-guide-to-coin-collecting/

https://www2.lawrence.edu/dept/art/BUERGER/ESSAYS/PRODUCTION3.HTML#:~:text=Ancient%20coins%20were%20made%20from,least%2020%20per%20cent%20silver.

https://www.thecollector.com/important-ancient-coins/

https://www.britannica.com/topic/coin-collecting/Modern-collecting

https://www.pcgs.com/top100

https://www.texmetals.com/news/what-is-the-difference-between-modern-and-vintage-coins/#:~:text=United%20States%20coinage%20can%20be,are%20usually%201965%20and%20after.

https://www.preciousmetals.com/blog/post/what-are-modern-coins.html

https://www.investopedia.com/terms/b/bullion-coins.asp

https://www.warwickandwarwick.com/news/guides/what-is-the-true-value-of-commemorative-coins

https://cosmosofcollectibles.com/what-is-the-difference-between-a-coin-a-commemorative-coin-and-a-medal/

https://www.atlantacutlery.com/american-revolution-coins

https://www.yoair.com/blog/what-are-pressed-pennies-and-collectible-medallions/

https://littlethings.com/lifestyle/pressed-pennies/3181271-2

https://www.fool.com/investing/general/2015/05/18/what-is-a-silver-certificate-dollar-worth.aspx

https://www.jmbullion.com/investing-guide/types-physical-metals/art-bars/

https://www.thesprucecrafts.com/coin-grading-services-768302#:~:text=A%20grading%20service%20or%20third,guaranteed%20that%20they%20are%20authentic.

https://www.thehealthyjournal.com/faq/can-you-get-a-coin-graded-for-free#:~:text=Grading%20prices%20vary%20according%20to,for%20%2465%20to%20%2480%20dollars.

https://www.thesprucecrafts.com/best-resources-for-coin-collectors-4685187

https://www.pcgs.com/services

https://www.goldeneaglecoin.com/foreign-coins--notes

https://www.bankrate.com/investing/worlds-most-valuable-coins/

https://topvegasbuyer.com/blog/foreign-coin-value-examined/

https://www.thesprucecrafts.com/coin-grading-made-simple-768384

https://www.warwickandwarwick.com/news/guides/coin-grading-guide

https://www.coinscarats.com/post/a-guide-to-coin-grading

https://libertycoinandcurrency.com/coins/foreign-coins/

http://coinmasters.net/coin-grade-buckets.html

https://www.sbcgold.com/investing-101/introduction-to-gold-coin-grading/

https://www.roslandgold.co.uk/blogs/blog/coin-grading-made-simple#:~:text=The%20Three%20Coin%2DGrading%20Buckets&text=Think%20of%20it%20as%20having,State%2C%20or%20MS)%20coins.
https://www.mintstategold.com/investor-education/cat/about-coin-grading/post/point-grading-scale/#:~:text=A%20Mint%20State%20(MS)%20coin,Business%20Strike%20coin%20can%20achieve.
https://www.ecwid.com/blog/how-to-sell-coins-online.html#:~:text=To%20make%20good%20money%2C%20start,or%20run%20your%20own%20website.
https://www.coinworld.com/voices/five_sure-five_ways.html
https://www.littletoncoin.com/LCC/html/pdf/how-to-collect-coins.pdf
https://catalogimages.wiley.com/images/db/pdf/9780470222751.excerpt.pdf
https://nashvillegoldandcoin.com/wp-content/uploads/2016/07/Buying__Selling_Guide.pdf
https://content.kopykitab.com/ebooks/2013/09/1984/sample/sample_1984.pdf
https://www.thesprucecrafts.com/strategies-for-investing-in-rare-coins-4142092
https://atlantagoldandcoin.com/identifying-the-best-times-to-sell-your-coin-collection/
https://www.pcgs.com/news/5-ways-to-determine-if-it-is-the-right-time-to-sell
https://www.thesprucecrafts.com/selling-coins-on-ebay-768231
https://www.websitebuilderexpert.com/building-online-stores/how-to-sell-coins-online/
https://www.ecwid.com/sell-coins-online
https://www.wikihow.com/Sell-Coins-on-eBay
https://www.henssler.com/how-to-sell-a-rare-coin-collection/
https://www.academia.edu/40942001/Taxation_on_Coin_Collectibles_Tips_for_Saving_Capital_Gains_Tax_on_Income_from_Sale_of_Coins
http://neilsberman.com/book/Chapter%203.pdf
https://www.investopedia.com/investing-in-rare-coins-5217604
file:///C:/Users/user/Downloads/csri-collectibles-2020.pdf
https://www.researchgate.net/publication/222025514_The_market_value_of_rarity/link/5c87989ba6fdcc88c39c3540/download
file:///C:/Users/user/Downloads/JEBORarity.PDF
https://www.blanchardgold.com/wp-content/uploads/2017/02/blanchard_lombra_report_2016.pdf
https://assetstrategies.com/PDF/Investing_In_Rare_Coins_Important_Facts.pdf
https://www.businesstoday.in/magazine/investment/story/rare-coins-paper-currencies-investment-portfolio-22694-2011-07-11
https://www.artincoins.com/
https://www.preciousmetals.com/blog/post/make-money-collecting-coins.html#:~:text=So%2C%20can%20you%20make%20money,coins%20you%20want%20to%20collect.
https://medium.com/@CanadianMint/thinking-of-becoming-a-coin-collector-here-are-5-simple-steps-to-get-you-started-ede92e4f1387
https://www.bullionbypost.co.uk/index/collectible-coins/coin-collector-name/
https://ncheteach.org/post/Common-Cents-Coins-as-Pedagogical-Tools

https://www.urbanpro.com/class-vi-viii-tuition/how-are-coins-a-valuable-source-of-information
https://www.prnewswire.com/news-releases/ancient-coins-for-education-puts-history-into-the-hands-of-children-96051974.html
https://www.archaeologyexpert.co.uk/ancientcoins.html
https://www.thesprucecrafts.com/coin-collecting-tips-for-beginners-768319
https://www.bnf.fr/en/how-catalogue-digitise-and-move-collection-coins-simple-tips
https://www.wikihow.com/Collect-Coins
https://www.bellevuerarecoins.com/the-different-ways-to-collect-coins/
https://www.preservationequipment.com/Blog/Blog-Posts/How-to-store-coins-full-guide#:~:text=Avoid%20areas%20of%20high%20humidity,easily%20stored%20in%20a%20safe.
https://www.usmint.gov/learn/collecting-basics/caring-for-your-coin-collection#:~:text=For%20high%2Dvalue%20coins%2C%20use,can%20ruin%20a%20coin's%20surface.
https://www.money.org/numismatic-blog/how-to-store-coin-collections
https://www.thesprucecrafts.com/top-ways-to-ruin-your-coins-768318
https://www.preciousmetals.com/blog/post/passing-down-your-coin-collection.html
https://numismatics.org/pocketchange/mint/
https://www.thesprucecrafts.com/what-is-a-mint-mark-768463
https://aggettainsurance.com/insurance-for-coin-collections-heres-what-you-need-to-know/
https://atlantagoldandcoin.com/the-dos-and-donts-of-selling-a-coin-collection-youve-inherited/
https://www.mintageworld.com/blog/numismatic-terminology/
https://www.investopedia.com/terms/d/denomination.asp#:~:text=Most%20often%2C%20a%20denomination%20is,such%20as%20government%2Dissued%20bonds.
https://www.investopedia.com/terms/m/mint.asp
https://www.mostrecommendedbooks.com/lists/best-coin-collecting-books
https://www.thesprucecrafts.com/reasons-to-start-collecting-coins-4589015
https://blog.feedspot.com/coin_forums/
https://www.thesprucecrafts.com/best-coin-collecting-software-5120712
https://www.thesprucecrafts.com/best-coins-sites-on-the-web-3898464
https://www.si.edu/spotlight/national-numismatic-collection
https://centurystamps.com/five-of-the-worlds-most-famous-coin-collections/#:~:text=1)%20National%20Numismatic%20Collection%2C%20Smithsonian,Smithsonian%20Institution%20in%20Washington%2C%20DC.
https://www.makeuseof.com/websites-buy-old-coins-banknotes/
https://www.streetdirectory.com/travel_guide/33995/hobbies/coin_dealer__get_to_know_the_secrets.html#:~:text=And%20they%20are%20the%20people,network%20of%20people%20seeking%20coins.
https://www.thesprucecrafts.com/tips-find-coin-dealer-768355

Made in the USA
Las Vegas, NV
13 November 2023

80778157R00157